BUCK TALES

Stories From the Deer Stand

JOE SHEAD

Contents

Part III Reflections

Part IV Bull Tales

About the Author

If you're looking for Joe Shead in spring or fall, check the woods. Shooting a 7-point buck during my first deer season had a profound impact on me. I tasted early deer hunting success and I wanted more!

My early years in the outdoors hunting and fishing would shape my whole life. I grew up in central Wisconsin at a time when deer numbers were robust on the private land I was fortunate enough to hunt. Outside of hunting season, I spent all my free time fishing. My time in the woods and on the water ultimately guided my career path.

I landed an internship at *Deer & Deer Hunting* magazine while in college. After college, I served as associate editor and ultimately managing editor at the magazine before moving on.

During my tenure at *D&DH*, I got heavily involved in shed hunting, ultimately writing a book on the subject. *Shed Hunting: A Guide to Finding White-Tailed Deer Antlers* continues to educate readers on this exciting pastime, now many years after its publication.

Now working as a freelance outdoor writer, I still write for *D&DH*, as well as several other publications. Stories from some of those publications are reprinted here.

I've been a storyteller since I was a boy. For me, telling stories about the hunt is every bit as important as venison on the table and time spent in the outdoors. I hope you enjoy my stories.

Introduction

For as long as there have been hunters, there have been hunting stories. Eons ago, killing animals was vital to survival. Prey species provided food, clothing and tools that were critical to sustaining the lives of ancient people. Today, we can always swing into the grocery store on the way home if our hunt is unsuccessful. Yet those cave-dwellers took time out of their lives – time that could have been devoted to acquiring more game or making useful tools – to draw their stories on cave walls. Although telling a hunting story wasn't necessary for their survival, they must have thought it was awfully important to take the time to draw pictographs of their hunt.

Today, we hunt for many reasons: food, camaraderie, relaxation, recreation and other reasons. But the story remains an important part of the hunt. Gather around a campfire at your deer camp or go out to the bar with your hunting buddies after a hunt, and inevitably, someone will start telling the story of their biggest buck or razz a hunting partner over a botched shot at a monster whitetail. Hunters are natural storytellers. It's likely something those of us who grow up in hunting families pick up listening to our elders tell stories of their own hunts when we're just children.

Indeed, some of our only memories of those who have gone before us may come from hunting tales. We may only know our grandfathers from a ragged deer head on the wall: ears torn, mouth sewn shut and eyes looking as if it were staring straight into a set of headlights. That mount and an old rifle in a caliber no longer made tucked somewhere safe in Dad's gun cabinet may be all that remains of a man we never met.

With a little prodding, maybe Dad could relate the story of Grandpa's big buck. Or the time Old Mossyhorns walked up on Uncle Lenny while he was taking care of his morning business. Or maybe Dad could explain just what kind of shenanigans was going on in the picture of him as a youth, sitting atop a frozen deer carcass as if he were riding a horse.

These stories transcend time and space. A good hunting story is just as entertaining today as it was when it was told in an old deer camp decades ago. Whenever hunters set out in search of wily whitetails, there are bound to be successes and failures … and stories with happy endings, disappointing finishes and just plain wacky misadventures.

For me, a good story is every bit as important as meat in the freezer and antlers on the wall. When I think about my own deer hunting stories, I lump them into three categories. The first variety is a good, old-fashioned deer hunt, where the pursuit of the deer is the main focus. Sometimes the hunt ends successfully; other times not. A deer doesn't always have to be killed to make a good story.

The second type of story is one in which the hunters take center stage. The deer play a necessary part, to be sure, but the friends and family members who were part of the hunt are the real takeaway.

Finally, the last kind of story is one where I sit back and reflect on the events of a hunt, sometimes years later, and I see it in a new light or give it a new spin. This tale isn't necessarily a narrative of an actual hunt. Rather, it looks at a hunt in an introspective, reflective manner. These tend to be my favorite stories.

In this book, I've assembled all three types of stories that I've experienced over my deer hunting career. These stories celebrate first deer, big bucks, little bucks, bucks that got away, friendships, high spirits and downright tragic moments. They really run the gamut of hunting emotions. Many of these tales were previously published in *Deer & Deer Hunting*, (Minnesota) *Outdoor News*, *Wisconsin Outdoor News* and *Northern Wilds*, and I thank these publications for allowing me to retell those stories here. Several of these stories are told here in print for the first time, although my friends and family are probably sick of me recounting these tales orally by now.

Whether you're a veteran hunter or a nimrod; a meat hunter or a trophy hunter, I hope you can relate to and enjoy these tales. We all hunt for different reasons, but in the end, our stories bind us together in the ancient fraternity of deer hunters. I hope you enjoy these tales as much as I've enjoyed telling them.

Acknowledgements

So many people have helped me write this book, whether they realize it or not. To all those who have latched onto an antler to help me drag a buck, I am deeply indebted. I also have to thank all those editors who considered my drivel worthy of print and any readers who have taken the time to let me know that someone is actually reading my work.

I want to call out my dad, first off. He's the one who took me hunting when I was a boy, and without him, I'd have never gotten so wrapped up in this outdoor lifestyle that I love so much. My first morning deer hunting with him, I sat inside a cardboard appliance box next to his plywood box stand. I watched Dad shoot a buck that morning and the excitement was contagious. Thanks, Dad, for introducing me to the outdoors.

I also thank my brothers James and Jack who accompanied me on many of my early hunts. It was always fun to pass the time in the deer stand with them and they played a key role in a lot of my early hunts.

George Piechowski owns the farm where I shot my first buck and found my first shed antler. Without his generosity to let my family hunt on his farm, especially in the 1990s when the deer population was burgeoning, I don't know that I'd have been so excited about deer hunting. It's a lot easier to enjoy hunting when you see dozens of deer each day, rather than freezing in a stand hoping to see just one on public land. So thanks George!

I've shared deer camps and enjoyed the hunt with many great hunting companions over the years. I really cherish the times when I've hunted with Ryan and Jen Bybee, Andy Lecker, Andy Chikowski, Aaron Opsteen and Andy Arens. Thanks for the companionship, deer dragging and great memories.

Thank you to the editors who allowed me to reprint several of my stories in these pages. Specifically, thanks to Dan Schmidt and Brad Rucks at Deer & Deer Hunting, Dean Bortz, Tim Spielman and Rob Drieslein at Outdoor News and Shawn Perich, Amber Pratt and Breanna Johnson at Northern Wilds.

I especially want to thank Kurt Mazurek for his amazing design skills. I came to him with an idea for how I wanted the book cover to look. He took the idea and ran with it and when it was done, I looked at it and thought, "I wouldn't have added these little touches, but I think that's exactly how it should look!" Kurt also did so many behind-the-scenes things that truly made the whole project come together. He does amazing work! Thanks Kurt!

Although my mom isn't a deer hunter, she's always been supportive of everything I've done, and I wouldn't be the person I am today without her. And although when she married my dad she said, "No deer heads on the wall!" she tolerated the mount of my first buck hanging proudly on the dining room wall for nearly 25 years before I finally brought it to my house! Thanks Mom!

And finally, thanks to Amanda Swanson for all her encouragement with the project and with her help getting it online and marketing this book. She's been a great companion on a few deer hunts as well and helps me in so many ways I don't even know where to start. Thanks Amanda!

Part I
Deer Hunts

My First Buck

For as long as I can remember, I'd been accompanying my dad on his frequent duck hunts. I stowed away in duck skiffs and knew how to paddle practically before I knew how to walk.

I first tagged along with him on a deer hunt in 1987 when I was 9, hunting on his friend George's farm. Dad's deer stand was a simple plywood box only 3 feet off the ground with barely enough room for one person. So on my first hunt, we built a wooden platform alongside the stand and I sat inside a giant cardboard washing machine box. I watched Dad shoot a buck opening morning and I was hooked! I couldn't wait until I was old enough to carry a gun and hunt for myself.

When I was finally old enough to carry my own gun, I had the deck stacked against me. I had to legally hunt within voice contact of Dad, so it made sense to sit with him, once again, in a cardboard box. Trouble was, Dad's stand is along a ditch at the corner of a cornfield and a fallow field. Most of his shots are 200 or 300 yards, which is no trouble for his scoped .270 Winchester. But those kind of shots were out of the question for me and my bead-sight 20-gauge shotgun.

I guess in my naïve excitement, I didn't consider that. I was just excited to be hunting!

On opening morning, we saw a 4-point buck walking across the field about 300 yards away. I don't know if Dad ever considered passing me his rifle or not. I'd never shot it before. I don't know if I'd ever even fired a scoped rifle. Honestly, I probably wouldn't have hit the deer, especially at that distance. Dad shot the buck and I was ecstatic. I don't recall being jealous; I was just thrilled that we'd gotten a buck.

On the second day, we were back in Dad's stand again. It amazes me, looking back, on how different deer hunting was in those days. Even at a young age, I knew that if you saw a buck, you shot it. I'd never heard of the concept of passing up a buck. If the people of Dad's generation had, none of them were practicing it on the farm we hunted.

Naturally, most of the bucks were killed on opening day. Sometimes hunters got lucky and shot a buck on the second day, but you seldom heard of anyone shooting a buck after that. And I'll never forget the year that David, George's brother-in-law, shot a 3-inch spike on the 8th day of our 9-day gun season. He was sitting way back in the swamp where all the wary bucks were surely hiding and he watched the deer for several minutes before he was confident the buck sporting a legally required 3-inch antler. At the time, I suggested someone call the local newspaper. People just didn't shoot bucks after opening weekend!

So there I was, on the second morning of deer season, hunting with my 20-gauge in a stand where long-range shots were the norm. Although we saw some does that morning, we didn't see anything with antlers, so I didn't have to worry about taking a shot.

At midday, we decided to try to find a buck hiding on some marshland my family has owned for generations. This land abuts a millpond and consists of cattails and alder, with a high spot in the middle. It's some thick, nasty cover that serves as the perfect refuge for deer under siege.

Dad posted me at the edge of the knoll where the high ground gives way to the marsh. George scaled one of two large oaks that serve as the only real trees among the brush. Dad and my 9-year-old brother, James, slogged through the thick alders rimming the knoll. After several minutes of fighting their way through the brush, the two orange blobs were nearing the end. George was already starting to free climb down from the big oak when the drivers kicked up a deer in the brush right behind me. Even though the deer passed me at only 20 yards, it was too brushy for me to see what it was. However, George managed to hold onto a branch and blaze away as a giant buck bounced across the cattail marsh. The buck escaped unscathed, but George couldn't believe the size of its rack. It had been years since he'd seen a buck like that.

When it was all over, George and Dad asked why I hadn't shot. I had no idea it was a buck. A running shot through the brush wasn't an ideal shot anyway; especially for a kid who had never even shot at a deer before.

I was obviously dejected as we climbed into Dad's truck. Even though I couldn't see the rack, I knew I'd missed my chance at a big buck.

After stopping for lunch, we headed back to George's farm, where several hunters were gathering at Big Joe's stand to do a deer drive. It was a 50-degree, bluebird day; not the type of weather you'd expect to see a deer out and about in the middle of the day. But as we drove down the farm road to meet the other drivers, Dad spotted a deer standing in a hayfield! Even at a couple hundred yards away, it was easy to see it was a buck!

Dad bailed out of the truck, intent on shooting the deer to fill my tag.

However, the buck had other ideas. When the truck stopped, the buck took off.

At this point, logically, Dad should have jumped back in the truck, but I'm guessing he must have had his gun out of the case already. So he jumped in the bed of the truck and yelled one word that I will never forget: "Drive!"

I'm sure this command must have surprised James and me, but it was obviously an urgent situation and we didn't question it. James was sitting in the middle seat, so he slid over into the driver's seat. Sometimes when we were cutting wood at my grandma's house, us kids would drive the truck for short distances to load and unload wood, so we did have a little driving experience. At 9 years old, however, James was having trouble reaching the pedals, so he steered while I ran the gas and brake from the middle seat. Thank God it was an automatic!

The buck sprinted the length of the hayfield, then dipped below a rise. James bounced along down the farm road paralleling the field while Dad hung on in the back. Seconds later, we dipped down the hill as well. The buck was gone, but in the distance, the neighbors were bailing out of their card shack like Paul Revere had announced that the British were coming! They lined up along the ditch that served as the property line, ready for war.

I braked to a stop. At the bottom of the hill, the hayfield flattened out, then extended another hundred yards to a strip of oak trees. This small section of trees wasn't more than 100 yards wide and consisted of mature oaks with little understory, so there wasn't a whole lot of cover. Beyond the oaks was 300 yards of picked cornfield, then the ditch where the neighbors stood lined up and ready.

"All right, let's be smart about this," Dad said as he jumped out of the truck bed. "Those guys must have seen the buck," Dad said, gesturing at the neighboring hunters. "There's only one place that deer can be. He's gotta be in the oak woods," Dad reasoned.

Dad jumped back in the truck and we drove to the far side of the oaks, but again, there was no deer in sight.

"All right," Dad began, "James, take the truck and drive over to Big Joe's stand where the guys are waiting. Tell them there's a buck in the woods and to drive it this way."

Dad and I exited the truck, then James drove away. I'm not sure how he managed to reach the pedals, but he did it. And I can only imagine the look on the faces of the grown men at Big Joe's stand when a 9-year-old boy came driving up in a pickup truck and told them what to do!

Dad and I stood in the field between the oaks and the ditch line where the neighbors waited. There was one red cedar tree at the edge of the oaks, and Dad speculated the buck was probably hiding under it.

The suspense was maddening. Would the guys listen to James? Would the buck run this way? There was nothing we could do but wait and hope the men did as James instructed.

Within minutes, I saw flashes of orange moving through the sparse trees. Suddenly, the buck burst from under the cedar tree, just as Dad predicted. He was actually running quartering toward us.

Dad's rifle cracked as the buck bounded across the field. I'm pretty sure, in my excitement, that the stock of the gun wasn't even fully against my shoulder when I touched off my first shot. The buck kept running, unscathed, as Dad fired again. I shot too, and still the buck kept coming at us.

After my second shot, time stood still. So many things happened in the matter of a second. I subconsciously remember hearing Dad's third shot, like a faraway echo in a dream. The buck was still running. Shotguns used for duck hunting cannot legally hold more than three shells. It's easy enough to take the plug out, and in doing so, my little 20-gauge was capable of holding five shells, but we hadn't bothered, never expecting I'd get or need five shots at a deer. In that split-second, I consciously recall knowing that I was down to my third and final shot. I swung the gun. I pulled the trigger. And the deer somersaulted to the ground.

"You got him!" Dad exclaimed. He slapped me on the back so hard, I literally almost fell over. My shot spined the deer and the buck was trying to regain his feet, but his hind end wasn't responding. "Reload and shoot him again," Dad instructed.

I did as told, then we excitedly approached the fallen buck. As I grasped his antlers, I saw him make his final twitch and then lie still.

The drivers, realizing they had succeeded, made their way over. And the neighbors burst across the property line, excited to see the deer up close. The deer was no giant, by any means. It was a 7-pointer. One of the brows had apparently broken off in velvet. The rack had a 15-inch spread. It was a nice deer, but back then, it was exceptional. People just didn't shoot anything bigger than a yearling in those days.

Before I knew it, I was surrounded by 20 hunters. I'd become almost an instant celebrity – the kid who shot the big buck. Many said I'd nev-

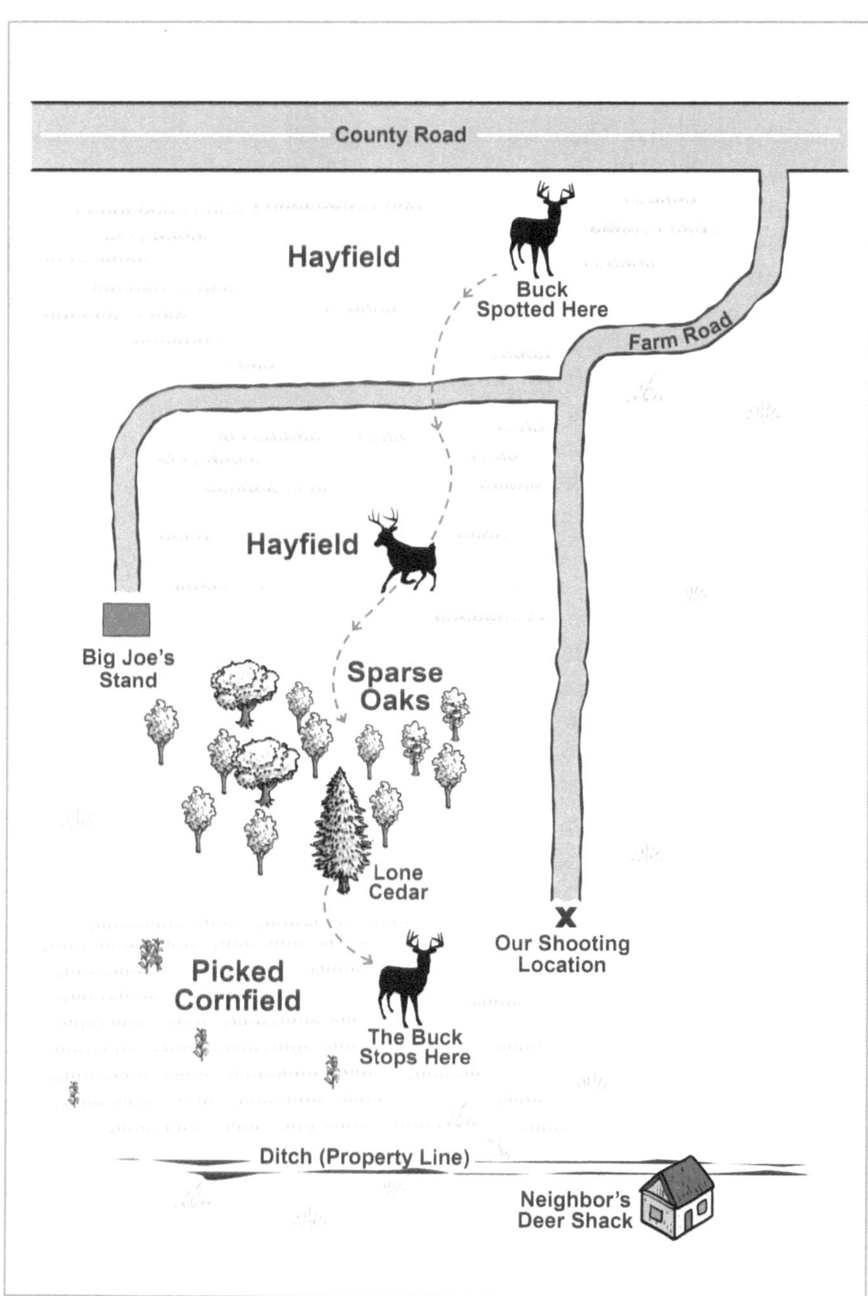

County Road
Hayfield
Buck Spotted Here
Farm Road
Hayfield
Big Joe's Stand
Sparse Oaks
Lone Cedar
Picked Cornfield
The Buck Stops Here
Our Shooting Location
Ditch (Property Line)
Neighbor's Deer Shack

I shot my first deer – a 7-pointer – on a crazy deer drive during my first season of hunting. That experience probably inspired my love for deer hunting.

er shoot a bigger one. That's how notable a buck like that was back in those days.

My head swelled far bigger than a kid's – or anyone's – ever should as I lavished in my triumph and my audience. Back home that night, I grabbed Dad's biggest rack off the wall. It fit right inside my buck's antlers. It was a pretty snotty thing for a kid to do!

Dad has always been a duck hunter, first and foremost, and deer season has always seemed like an annoying obligation to try to fill the freezer when he'd rather be chasing waterfowl. I love duck hunting too. But tasting deer hunting success at such a young age changed me. There's just something about wrapping your hands around a set of antlers that I can't get from duck hunting.

The Texas Heart Shot

Opening day of Wisconsin's 1996 deer season started off innocently enough. But as the season dawned on opening morning, little did I know that the day's events would teach me a life-long lesson ... and leave my head spinning.

It snowed opening morning. Most deer hunters would be excited to see snow, which makes it easier to spot deer and follow tracks and blood trails. The snow had a big impact on my family. My dad plowed snow for the county highway department for more than 30 years, so he was in a plow truck, rather than a deer stand, opening morning. So my brother, James, and I rode together to the Piechowski farm where we hunted without Dad.

Deer were plentiful in Wisconsin's farm country during the mid-'90s. I don't remember how many deer I saw that morning. Heck, looking back, I wish I'd kept a tally of how many deer I used to see on all my hunts back in the good old days. Deer numbers now are well short of what they used to be, even in farm country, and the guys who still hunt that farm see only a fraction of the deer that they used to. But back then it was nothing to see 40 deer or more each day.

I'm sure I probably saw quite a few deer that morning, but the only one I remember was a wide-racked 8-pointer. My stand was just a plywood box on the ground along a fence line. At my back was a harvested crop field. In front of me was a cow pasture. About 175 yards across the pasture was a finger from a large tamarack swamp that spanned four properties. The swamp was the perfect sanctuary for deer, and with ample food in the fields and plenty of cover, there were literally hundreds of deer in the area!

In front of my stand, the swamp tapered down to a point, which was surrounded by pasture on my side and another picked field on the other. Another box blind overlooked the opposite side of the finger. That's where the landowner's nephew, Dan, sat. His stand was always productive.

I don't remember the time, but somewhere around mid-morning, that wide 8-pointer popped out of the tamarack finger. He jumped the fence into the pasture and was more or less walking right at me, although his direction of travel would carry him about 100 yards to my right. I just let him come. He was walking briskly, no doubt looking for does, and besides, he was getting closer the whole time. I'd just let him keep coming and when he got broadside, I'd shoot.

The buck was getting closer and closer, but suddenly my plan fell apart. Dan always parked his truck right along the same fence line where my blind was situated, about 100 yards straight to my right. Suddenly spotting the parked vehicle, the buck slammed on the brakes. The pasture was wide open – save for two cedar trees – and just my luck, the buck happened to stop right behind one of those cedars. There he was, standing only 125 yards away in an open pasture, and I didn't have a shot!

The buck sized up the truck for a couple seconds, then did an about face and bounded back toward the swamp. I shot once, but I had no idea where to aim at a leaping deer. I watched in despair as the buck jumped the fence and disappeared back into the swamp.

I was crestfallen! The buck looked like a giant to me, and what an accomplishment it would have been to tag him! I was only a freshman in college and I was hungry to prove myself as a deer hunter.

I stared at the swamp, not wanting to let the buck get away. The neck of the swamp was only about 75 yards wide. Maybe 200 yards from the point of the finger, a road cut diagonally through the trees. Although it would have been a very long, difficult shot to shoot at a deer crossing the road, I could at least see the road from my stand and I knew the buck hadn't crossed it. And Dan hadn't shot, so I knew the buck was still in the last digit of that swampy finger.

I was still staring at the road minutes later when I saw orange materialize to my right. Dan had obviously heard me shoot and was walking around the point of the swamp to see if I had a deer. I frantically waved at him, doing the best I could to show big antlers on my head with my hands, trying to get him to go back to his stand. After some frantic waving, he finally got the drift and retreated to his stand, but about that time, the commotion must have been too much and I saw the buck streak across the road bisecting the swamp.

It was over and I'd blown my chance at a nice buck.

At lunchtime, I walked back to the farmhouse to relate my tale. Dad was there now, his roads cleared for the day. He was upset that I'd botched my chance at the buck. But no one was more disappointed than me.

Heading back out to sit that afternoon was deflating. I felt like a batter who had just crushed a baseball that had plenty of homerun distance, but arced just foul. Now I had to start from scratch. I'd probably never see that buck alive again.

My stand is a great place to intercept deer as they move to and from farm fields to feed, but it's usually pretty quiet during the middle of the day. The sun was out now and it just didn't seem like a productive place to sit. So I hatched an idea where I could ambush that buck. I highly doubted if he'd come back out in the open again during daylight, especially after he'd been shot at. So I decided to hunt from the ground where the swamp tapered down, right near the road bisecting the tamaracks.

The Piechowskis are beekeepers, and there are always random bee frames, called "supers," lying around. They make perfect seats. Someone had obviously hunted inside that finger once before and I found a single super in the woods, which became my perch for the evening.

I plopped down on the bee box, facing my deer stand, which was straight north. I was positioned right along the southern edge of the tamarack finger, so any deer that crossed the finger would be to the north. At my back was a small fallow field consisting of goldenrod and then a plowed field beyond that. No way would any deer cross that open country. They would certainly walk through the tamarack strip.

Dad's stand was along the intersection of two drainage ditches out in the middle of crop fields. It was always a good spot on opening morning, but once the jig was up, the only deer you saw there were far away and often on the run. So Dad positioned himself further into the swamp. He was actually only a couple hundred yards away, overlooking the only other logging road that cut across the swamp. That spot, at the corner of the swamp and pasture, was always a great spot. The guy who used to hunt there sometimes saw 100 deer a day. No exaggeration!

Dad's plan, like mine, was to intercept the big buck as it came out of the swamp. I didn't think about it at the time, but Dad was actually kind of cutting me off in that spot, positioned at the north edge of the swamp, but farther to the east.

I sat slumped on the bee box, dwelling on my missed opportunity. Chances at big bucks don't come often. It could be years before I got another opportunity.

I'd been sitting on that box for more than an hour. Not once did I swivel my head to look behind me. There was no need. The deer would come from my right, from deep within the swamp, and head to my left to enter the ag fields around dusk. It was pretty simple. But after sitting there for more than an hour, suddenly, one of those funny feelings told me to turn around right now!

I spun just in time to see a buck – *the* buck – crossing behind me, loping through the goldenrods and heading for the wide-open field, at least an hour before dark!

By the time I saw him, he was already past me. I whirled around and shouldered my rifle. He was cruising at a brisk walk, just about straight away, only 60 or 70 yards away.

There wasn't much of a shot opportunity, but I'd read something in a magazine about the "Texas heart shot." If you hit the deer right at the base of the tail, you'd spine the deer, dropping him in his tracks. So I put the crosshairs on the buck's tail and fired. The buck bolted and was out of sight in seconds.

I hurried to where the buck had been when I shot. He hadn't dropped on the spot like he was supposed to, but there was blood in the snow. The deer was headed toward the open field, so I expected to see him somewhere, but there was no buck in sight. I took up the blood trail in the snow immediately. Somehow, the deer had managed to stay concealed in the goldenrods. I don't know how I hadn't seen him. He hooked in an arc and once again had taken a 180 from his original direction of travel. He was heading back for the main body of the swamp!

As soon as I realized that, I got off the track, circled to the north and made a beeline toward Dad. Yes, he'd seen the buck zip across the logging road heading toward me a few minutes before he heard me shoot, but it was gone before he could even raise his gun.

I relayed my story, all the while watching the logging road, not Dad. The buck was circling back to the swamp. I told Dad to be ready for him. I'd get back on the track. I'd either catch up with the buck, or Dad could shoot him when he crossed the logging road.

I took up the track again. The buck was headed right for the blazed road through the swamp. We had him now! Any moment, Dad would put him down. But I tracked the buck right to the road, and the tracks simply crossed. He'd slipped through without being seen! I couldn't believe it.

Although the buck's primary direction of travel was east, he was also moving south. He was probably 250 or 300 yards south of Dad's position when he crossed that road. Eventually, he angled toward the drainage ditch on the south edge of the property. He crossed the ditch onto the neighbor's land.

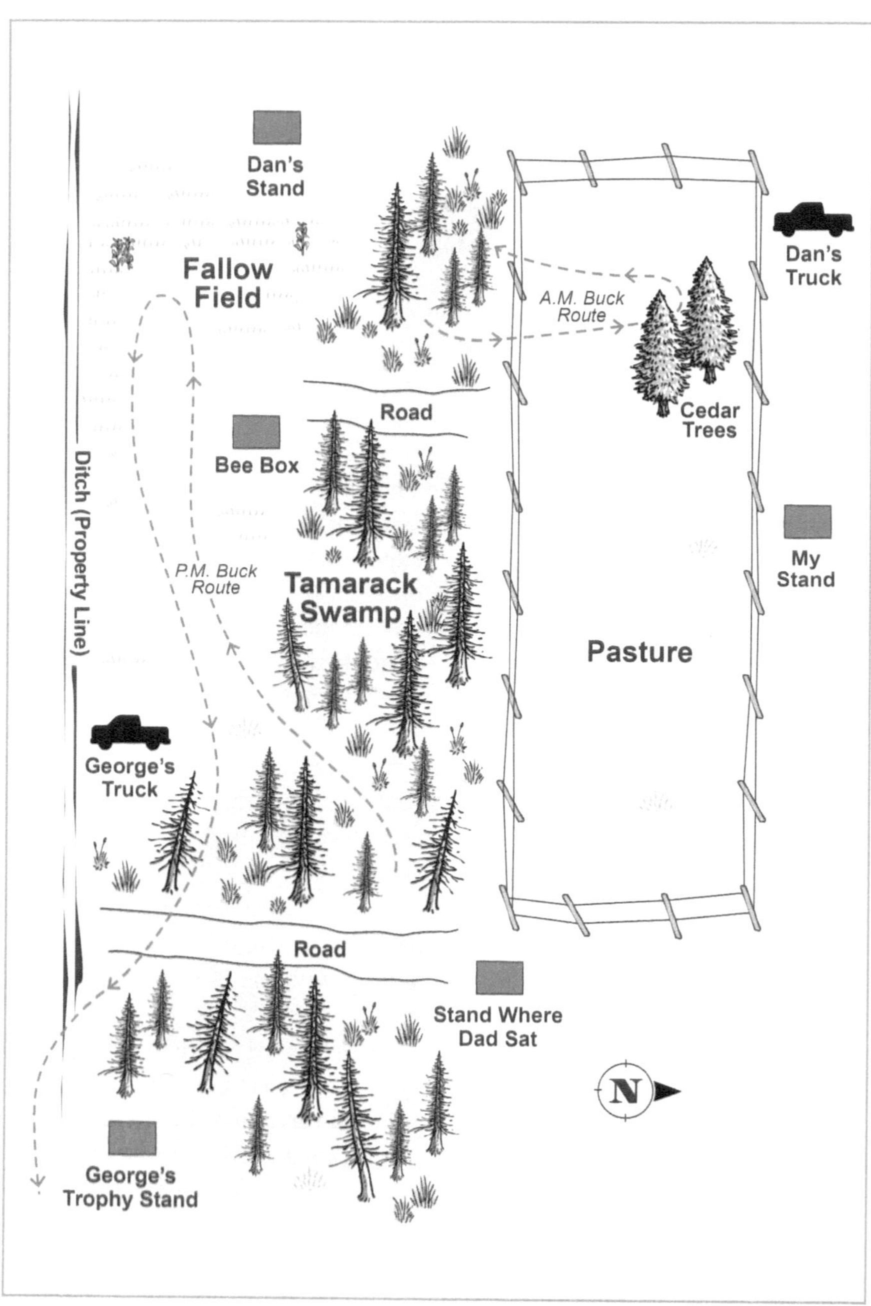

Dan's Stand
Fallow Field
Ditch (Property Line)
Bee Box
Road
A.M. Buck Route
Dan's Truck
Cedar Trees
My Stand
P.M. Buck Route
Tamarack Swamp
Pasture
George's Truck
Road
Stand Where Dad Sat
N
George's Trophy Stand

I was sick. I was completely helpless. I'd now taken a bad shot and wounded a deer and there was nothing I could do. As bad as it was missing the buck in the morning, wounding him and having him cross onto the neighbor's land was even worse.

It was time to get George. George owns the farm and knows the neighbors. His stand, "George's Trophy Buck Stand," was positioned just north of the southern edge of his property, but deeper into the swamp. I walked east along the ditch that designates the property line to get George. Sheepishly, I approached George, who was trying to hunt on opening afternoon of deer season. I hated to bother him, but what could I do?

George left his stand and walked with me back to where I'd left the buck's track. As we approached the ditch, the buck jumped up from his bed on the other side.

"Geez, that thing is wide!" George gasped.

George crossed the ditch onto the neighbor's land. I stayed behind, now totally powerless to do anything about the messy situation I'd created.

I was sick. What should I do? I didn't feel like hunting. I walked west along the drainage ditch to where George parks when he's hunting. From there, I cut across the open field, back to the bee box. I didn't know what else to do. As I sat on the bee box, I replayed the scene over and over in my mind. It was incredible to me that a buck that was clearly old enough to know better would exit the swamp a second time during daylight. I looked at the area where the buck had crossed in the afternoon. It wasn't a long shot. But the Texas heart shot leaves little room for error. If you miss that narrow spine, at best you'll hit ham, which will only wound a deer. I vowed to never take that shot again.

But right now, I had to deal with the consequences. I beat myself up over the way things had unfolded. I'd been lucky that my plan had actually worked. It was a great audible. It's just that the execution was lacking.

I paced back and forth, chastising myself. I wasn't hunting anymore; I was just standing in the woods with a gun. Dad had returned to his post at the north edge of the swamp. James was sitting in his stand back in the swamp with no idea of what had happened. And somewhere, across the ditch, George was trailing a punk teen's buck when he could have been sitting in his stand on opening day.

The minutes crawled by. I suppose I could have left. James could have gotten a ride with Dad, but this was before any of us had cell phones and there was no way to communicate that. So I stayed.

Periodically, shots echoed in the distance. Then, right before dark, shots rang out in the swamp, not that far back. It was about quitting time anyway, so I walked back to where George and Dad had parked their trucks along the ditch, curious to find out if someone in our party had killed a deer.

No one was at the vehicles or even within sight. I began walking along the ditch on the property line where I'd inevitably run into someone coming out of the woods. Although my stomach was still in knots, the possibility that someone else may have shot a deer at least took away a little of my anguish.

It was now dark, and I still hadn't run into anyone exiting the woods. Someone must have gotten a deer!

I was almost to George's Trophy Buck Stand when I finally saw two hunters walking toward me along the ditch. It was James and Dad.

"Come on," Dad said as he turned to walk back into the swamp.

Now I was thoroughly confused. Someone must have shot a deer!

We hiked a couple hundred more yards into the swamp. Although the trail is good up to George's stand (and on dry years he can get a tractor back there) beyond that, the trail narrows and becomes more rugged. Only deer maintain it.

Finally, up ahead, a light shone. It had to be George, but I struggled to see what he was doing.

I hurried forward, now really anxious to find out what was going on. George was standing over the wide-racked 8-pointer!

"Who shot him?" I asked.

"Someone with a .270," Dad replied. That wasn't much help. Between the four of us, George was the only one who didn't shoot a .270 Winchester.

The guys played me for a while. Finally, George spilled the story. He'd taken up the track of the buck after it crossed the ditch onto the neighbor's land. The buck was moving along steadily, but was limping because I'd shot him in the right ham, inches to the right of where I'd aimed. George tracked the deer right past another young hunter who shot at it one time.

"Did you get him?" George asked the young man, who was perched in a tree.

"I didn't shoot," the teen replied. He was so rattled by the buck that he had no recollection of even shooting, even though George clearly heard him shoot!

George stayed on the track. The deer kept bleeding and between the blood and the deer's limping tracks, he was easy to follow in the new

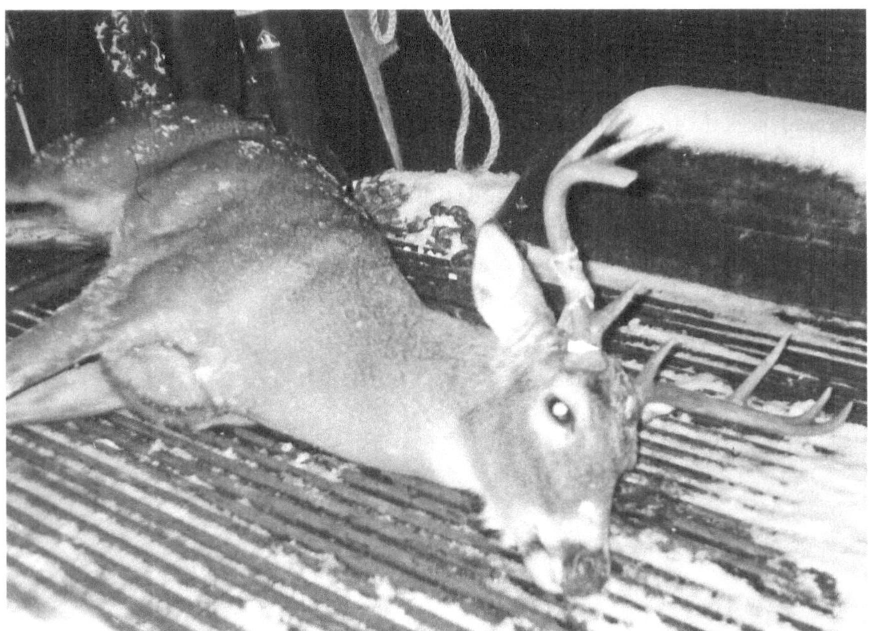

I got two chances at this 8-pointer in the same day. After I took a questionable shot, this buck led the landowner onto the neighbor's property and then back onto his own before my dad finally put the buck down.

snow. A couple different times, George glimpsed the deer up ahead, but couldn't get a shot.

All the while, the buck was circling back, heading north, back toward the ditch and George's property. Finally, George got close enough to the buck that he got a crack at the deer, but he missed. Eventually, the buck crossed the ditch back to George's land.

Meanwhile, Dad and James had been about ready to leave their stands when they heard George shoot, so they headed into the swamp to see if he needed help. Dad and James were walking side by side along the ditch when they saw a deer walking right at them. Dad shot, dropping the buck in its tracks.

What a whirlwind of emotions! It seemed like it had been days since my first encounter with the buck earlier that morning. Despite all that had happened, it was over. I didn't have to worry about a wounded deer struggling to survive. That was a huge weight off my chest. More than 25 years have passed and I've never tried the Texas heart shot again and I never will. I have too much respect for deer to try that.

But then the question was, whose deer was it? Dad killed it. George tracked it. I'd only wounded it. Dad and George graciously let me tag it. If I hadn't hit the deer and created a blood trail, none of that wild story would have happened. I was excited to claim him, but I felt sheepish that I'd put everyone through such an ordeal. The 8-pointer had short tines, but an impressive 18-inch inside spread. He'd taken us on a roller coaster ride and I'm sorry he suffered for hours on three good legs. But I'm thankful it worked out in the end.

50 Deer at Once

A perfect storm was brewing during Wisconsin's 2000 deer season. After a few years of mild winters, the deer herd was burgeoning. Crops were coming off on schedule, taking away cover that could hide deer in farmland areas. And the weather during the opening weekend of gun season was perfect. There was snow on the ground, which helps hunters spot deer and follow blood trails. And with temperatures in the 20s, it was cold enough to get deer moving, but still tolerable for most hunters.

My family had the incredible good fortune of hunting on a friend's 400-acre farm in central Wisconsin. It had the best deer hunting I'll probably ever see. The farm fields held all the food deer could need. But what really made the place a deer haven was a miles-long tamarack swamp that spread over four properties, providing ample cover.

"Spoiled" might be the word that best describes hunting on the Piechowski farm. Deer numbers were downright ridiculous! Only one person bow-hunted the property. During gun season, hunters were strategically set up over farm fields, cow pastures, an oak forest, red willow brush and in the tamarack swamp. The hunters pinballed deer back and forth, so deer were frequently on the move. On any given day during deer season, I'd usually see about 40 deer from my simple box blind on the ground in a cow pasture, facing the tamarack swamp. On my best day ever, I counted a staggering 172 deer!

Despite the incredible deer numbers, we could have done a better job of managing the property. We seldom shot does. And when I first started hunting, you just shot any buck you saw. By the mid-1990s, we were passing up yearling bucks – if we felt like it. I don't like rules governing what you can and cannot shoot. I feel that self-imposed rules cause tension between hunters. But certainly with restraint on young buck harvest, combined with a managed doe harvest, that place could have produced some big bucks. But it was a family farm. In fact, my family members were the outsiders. We were the only ones hunting during gun season who weren't related to the landowner, so who were we to tell him how to run things? We were plenty thrilled with the opportunities we had.

Gun season in Wisconsin always starts the Saturday before

Thanksgiving and runs through Thanksgiving weekend. After opening weekend that year, my dad, my two brothers and I all still had our buck tags. The funny thing is, despite all the deer running around, we seldom shot anything after opening weekend. So our Thanksgiving morning hunt that year was mostly a formality.

The plan Thanksgiving morning was to hunt a few hours, then make the 5-minute drive to my aunt and uncle's place for a noon dinner. Despite the fact that four of us toted rifles to the farm that morning, none of us really expected to shoot a buck.

Dad would be in his ground stand on the west end of the farm. His stand is a great opening day spot, when deer are going about their normal routine of feeding in the field at night before retreating into cover for the day. In fact, he had an incredible record of seeing a buck on opening day every year he hunted that stand. However, once the lead started flying, deer preferred to stay tighter to cover and his stand became less productive.

My brother, James, would sit in his tripod stand deep in the tamarack swamp, where deer felt safer moving around during daylight hours. Still, once the pressure was on, they tried to lay low in the swamp.

My brother, Jack, decided to sit with me in my box stand between the cow pasture and a crop field, and only about 175 yards from the tamarack swamp. This decision was probably made in no small part because he had shot his first buck from my stand the year before. We were usually treated to a parade of deer leaving the fields and heading for cover in the morning in that spot. Of course, if hunters were driving the oak woods or somehow got deer moving elsewhere on the farm, there was always a chance we might see them in the open pasture, heading for the swamp. Often, if they were undisturbed, we'd spot them milling around just inside the tamaracks. It seemed there was always something to watch in the morning.

So Jack and I sat in the simple plywood ground blind as the curtain came up Thanksgiving morning. As I reflect back on that stand, some things were always the same. The Piechowskis raise Simmental beef cattle, and one year a cow died right near the box blind. For as long as I hunted after that, the skull was always there, slowly being reclaimed by the elements.

Also, each morning, I'd watch the headlights of a hunter on the neighboring property slicing through the darkness. I'd see his lights flicker as they alternately appeared behind and in front of the sparse trees in the mature forest. Then the hunter spun a 180 and parked. I always noted the spot where the lights went out in case I ever got a shot in that direction, even though he parked a half-mile away.

One of my favorite aspects of hunting are those quiet moments in the darkness, minutes before the grayness of dawn. At that moment, anything is possible. In a half-hour, you may see the biggest buck of your life. In a couple hours you may be at the check station, telling and re-telling the story of how you killed your deer. There are no thoughts of being cold or anxiety over missed shots or blown opportunities. It's peaceful and exciting.

Jack and I sat, watching the sun rise over some incredible deer hunting grounds. We saw several does and fawns during that first magic hour, but it's amazing how skewed the buck-to-doe ratio was on that farm. On my record-setting day when I saw 172 deer, only seven of them sported antlers.

By mid-morning, we hadn't seen a buck and deer movement had slowed. However, unbeknownst to us, some of the hunters in the swamp were getting restless. The landowner, George, sits far back in the swamp, and toward mid-morning he often decides to "take a little walk." As you can imagine, given the sheer number of deer taking refuge in the tamaracks, his walks always get deer moving. Our brother James decided to stretch his legs about the same time.

Back in the box blind, Jack and I had no idea George and James were on the move. We just sat, now talking more and watching for deer less as the sun inched higher in the sky.

As we sat, a brown blob appeared about 500 yards away on the neighbor's property. I raised my binoculars, but even before I did so, I realized I was looking at several deer exiting the tamaracks and crossing some open marsh grass. More and more of them spilled out of the swamp, stringing out single file across the grass. They advanced north until one of them must have seen the truck parked in the oak trees. Now the entire herd stood in the open grass, unsure of how to proceed. Through binoculars I counted the deer as they strung out across the marsh, then balled up in confusion. Twenty-five deer stood in a pile! It's probable there were some small bucks in the herd, given the sheer number of deer, but no large racks jumped out at me at that distance.

Suddenly, I caught motion in the corner of the cow pasture, much closer than the deer in the marsh grass. In that corner of the pasture, tamaracks had spilled across the fence line and grew for a few yards into the pasture. To the south of the fence corner lay the tamarack swamp. East of the fence

I have many great memories of my box blind in the cow pasture. Herds of deer regularly passed through the pasture as they traveled between crop fields and the tamarack swamp in the background.

was the neighbor's property where the herd of 25 deer stood.

By the time I raised my rifle to scope the deer in the pasture corner, the aperture was filled with deer!

"Here come some on ours," I excitedly whispered as deer exited the swamp and ducked under or jumped over the fence.

The new herd of deer crossed the line fence, then strung out along a perpendicular fence, paralleling our position. I counted them as they crossed the fence … 25 deer in this herd too! And I could still see the 25 deer on the neighbor's property, still trying to decide whether to keep moving toward the parked truck or to double back toward the hunters who had obviously disturbed them. Fifty deer within sight, all at once!

"There's a buck, Jack," I said. "Oh, there are a couple bucks!"

As the deer strung out along the fence, we scanned for antlers. Three of them were bucks. None of them were big. In fact, they were a pretty sad lot, but we decided to shoot.

Jack claimed the biggest one, which sported two points on one side but had broken off his other antler. I called dibs on the spike. I had always been fascinated with those meager, unbranched racks. But although I'd

This odd buck carried a single spike on one side and a ball of antler on the oppo-site pedicle. The buck dressed at 163 pounds. Why it grew such small, deformed antlers is a mystery.

heard of guys shooting spike bucks, I'd never seen one until now. In fact, I had once told some friends I wanted to shoot a buck with 3-inch spikes (in Wisconsin, a deer has to have at least one 3-inch antler to be considered a legal buck) and do a European mount. I always thought those small spike racks were so cool!

With a plan in place for who would shoot which deer, we waited to make sure the deer were clear of other deer, then I told Jack to shoot when he was ready. Jack shot, and at the report, I fired too.

You can imagine the pandemonium of 25 deer scattering in every di-rection after gunfire erupts. It was sheer chaos! Jack's buck was down, but was flailing as it struggled to jump the fence. A follow-up shot put it down for keeps.

Then there was the question of my buck. I thought I saw it jump the fence, but it was hard to be sure. Jack and I exited the stand and walked the 175 yards to look for our deer. We found Jack's buck piled up by the fence. As he began field dressing his deer, I walked the wide trail along the fence, looking for blood in the snow. To my delight, I soon found a blood trail. The trail was easy to follow in the fresh snow. I hoped it would be a

Jack and I pose with our meager bucks. Jack shot a 2-point buck that carried only one antler and I shot a spike with just one antler. Another spike among the herd of 25 deer got away.

short trail with a dead buck at the end.

As I tracked the deer, I saw faded orange coming through the woods. Only George wore blaze orange that faded. He'd heard the shooting and was coming to investigate. I trailed the deer as George approached. Soon, I spotted brown fur up ahead where my deer lay still. I reached it only 30 seconds before George did. But as I walked up to it, something wasn't right. There were no antlers sticking up! Granted, I knew I was shooting at a spike, but there should have been something sticking up besides ears. I couldn't believe it! I must have mistakenly killed a doe!

Legally I wouldn't be in any trouble. Deer numbers were so high back then you automatically got a doe tag with your buck tag. But we generally didn't shoot does at George's. It was definitely frowned upon. There was no hiding my mistake. George was mere yards away and closing fast. What was I going to tell him?

I knelt down in the snow next to the deer as George walked up to me. What was this? A single spike antler protruded from the buck's skull, and of course that was the side that was buried in snow! That was a relief! At least I'd killed a buck! On the upper side, there was a ball of antler on the pedicle. That's it. It was an odd-looking deer.

The kicker was, when I was watching the deer before we shot, there was definitely a spike in the herd with antlers on each side. Jack and I had killed two ugly halfracks sporting a whopping 3 points between them and my dream spike buck had slipped away!

I don't know what happened to my oddball buck. It wasn't a young deer. Later, it would dress out at 163 pounds. But for whatever reason, it didn't grow much of a rack.

As we gathered around our bucks, James showed up as well. The swamp sitters hadn't coordinated their walks, but they sure got the deer moving that morning, just by dumb luck. Although the quality of the bucks was poor, I'll never forget seeing 50 deer at once while deer hunting!

The Millpond Buck

We didn't know it at the time, but the first time we ever tried the millpond drive, we executed it to perfection. Well, almost. The drive was over for all practical purposes when a huge buck burst from the brush mere yards from me and tore down the hill and across the surrounding marsh amidst a barrage of lead. Our primary stander was hanging from a limb half-way down from his perch in a giant oak, and despite the fact the buck was practically under my feet, as a rookie deer hunter, I never saw its antlers as it bounded through the thick cover. That drive has never worked quite the same since.

The millpond drive takes place on an 18-acre slice of marsh. My great-grandpa, a dyed-in-the-wool duck hunter, lived in an old blue trailer here with an outhouse out back. Before he died, the rumor goes he sold the land jointly to his two grandsons for $1 apiece. Legend also states that he loaned my dad the dollar.

The land is arranged beautifully; almost in a manner in which you could capitalize on a nervous deer's escape route. And sometimes we do. Problem is, we rarely have doe tags for the area, and usually only does run out "like they should."

The millpond abuts the north end of the property. The land is completely marsh, made up of cattails, tag alders and other muddy, boot-sucking boggy vegetation, except near the road and on "the knoll."

The knoll is what makes the drive possible. It's the perfect deer sanctuary. Situated on the north end of the property, nestled against the pond, the high, open ground of the knoll gives deer a commanding view of their surroundings. Deer will hear and see you if you come across the marsh toward them, and they'll probably smell you if you come at them from the pond. There simply is no way to sneak up on them.

Rimming the knoll is a thick layer of alders, on the transition between moist and dry ground. It is here that deer lie, plotting their escape around the sloshing driver.

The driver – usually me – heads straight north from the road. The standers post down in the marsh to the southeast where the good walking

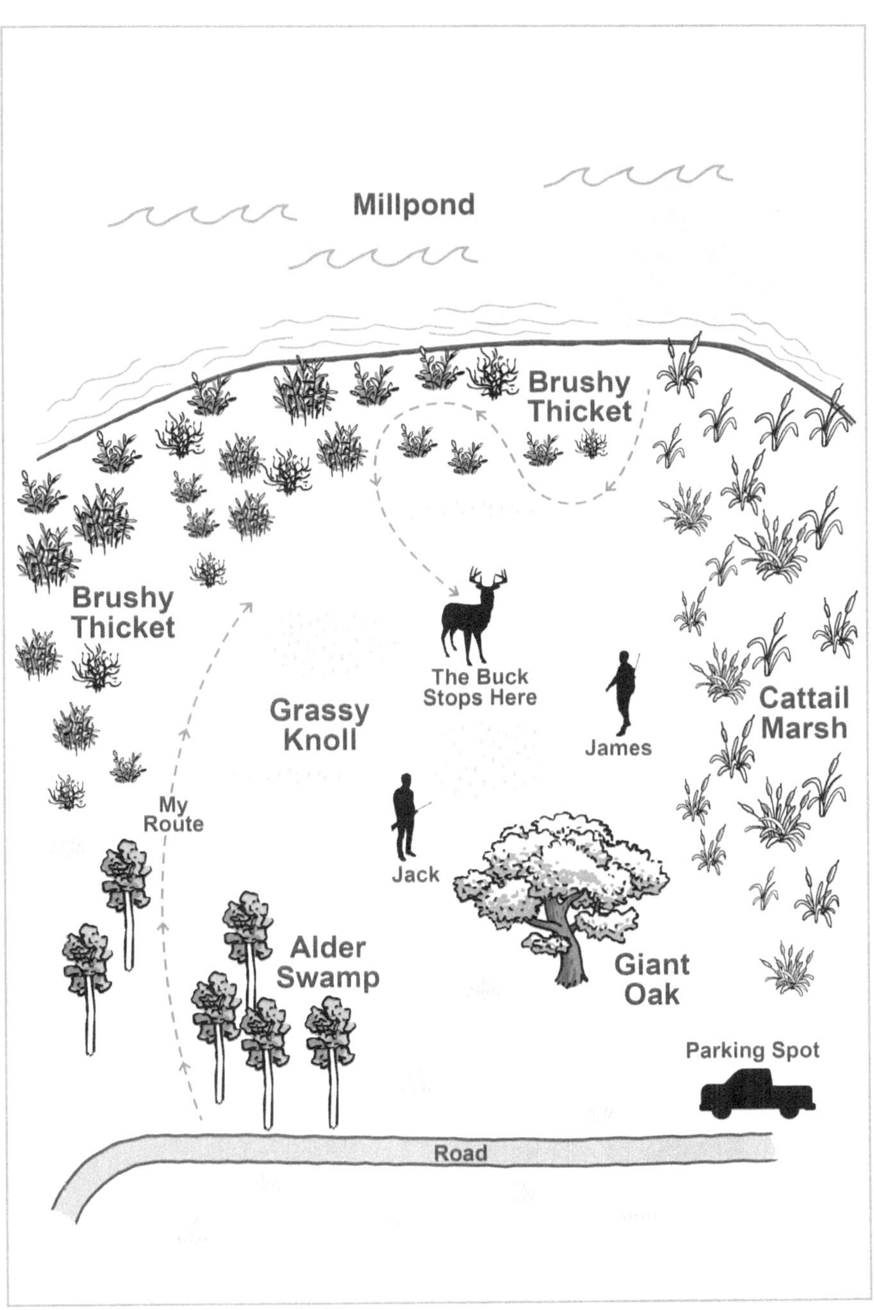

Millpond
Brushy Thicket
Brushy Thicket
Cattail Marsh
Grassy Knoll
The Buck Stops Here
James
My Route
Jack
Alder Swamp
Giant Oak
Parking Spot
Road

gives way to the bad. It is helpful to have a duck hunting upbringing to be the driver. It is the only activity I know of that gives you the confidence to leap from alder bog to alder bog across waist-deep water. Even while wearing waders, I rarely make it to the knoll still dry.

Meanwhile, back on the good walking, the posters stand yawning, wondering when (and if) that slowpoke driver is gonna make it to the knoll. The deer never get up until the end of the drive, which takes a good 45 minutes to complete.

The driver ambles his way to that big oak, then heads west, then north and finally back to the east as he circles the knoll's rim. The standers ready themselves because only the deer know which way they'll run. One year a buck ran across the frozen pond. Another time, a spike buck ran to the base of the knoll and saw my 13-year-old brother standing 50 yards away. The buck was standing broadside, but it wasn't to be Jack's first buck.

Another time, during an antlerless-only hunt, I rousted a wide-racked, pot-bellied buck who was in no hurry to escape as he trotted across the wide-open knoll. I stood powerless and dumbfounded 30 yards away.

In 2001, a new chapter began at the millpond. That summer, my dad's cousin sold his share of the property, giving my family sole ownership of the land. That made the 2001 drive special.

My brothers and I decided to make the drive on the seventh day of Wisconsin's 9-day gun season. We don't often disturb the area in fall, essentially turning the knoll into a deer sanctuary.

As usual, I opted to be the driver. James posted atop the knoll and Jack stood in the marsh down below. By the time I reached the knoll, I had a boot full of water and I was stripping layers fast. I began circling the knoll, first heading west, then returning back near the big oak. I was nearly three-quarters finished and had heard no shooting or crashing through the brush. Still, I remained ready. I had learned that deer often bed just northeast of the oak.

One hundred yards from the endpoint, I saw antlers. A small buck found its feet and cut back across the knoll and dashed into the alders on the north side from where I'd just emerged. James could have shot, but he was waiting for a trophy. Jack and I were only looking for antlers. James made a beeline for the west end of the knoll. Here, there was a small gap in the brush, and we didn't see the deer run across the opening. I waved Jack to the top of the knoll. After informing him of the situation, he stood in the center of the knoll and I posted on the east end at the edge of the brush.

James, myself and Jack put together a drive that outwitted this spike buck. It was the first buck we killed on that drive in a dozen years of trying.

Unless the buck had pulled a Houdini act, it was sandwiched in a strip of brush 100 yards long by 20 yards wide. On the north end was the pond and on the south end was the open knoll. James and I flanked the west and east ends, respectively. If the buck was indeed in the brush, its only chance of escaping was to swim across the pond.

James entered the brush, disappearing and reappearing according to the thickness of the cover. My mind raced. Would the buck swim for it? Were we set up OK? Could the deer get past me? My heart hammered in my ears as only it can when I know I'm about to encounter game. When James was halfway through, the buck sneaked to the edge of the brush and stopped 30 yards from me. It was then, I think, when it saw me that it realized it was trapped. The buck paused, then bolted into the open, pitting its only hope of survival in the chance Jack and I would miss. The buck split between Jack and me, and for a moment all we could do was watch. As the buck cleared Jack, I found it in my scope. I swung hard and slapped the trigger as the buck disappeared over the crest of the knoll.

For a moment I didn't know what had happened. Did I miss? Could we have adjusted so perfectly to the circumstances, only to blow it?

Was the deer wounded? If it made it into the marsh, it would be a nightmare to track.

Jack answered my question when he snapped his rifle to his shoulder to finish the spine-shot buck.

It was a moment of triumph. Three boys had done what grown men had not accomplished in a dozen years of trying. As we gathered around the fallen spike, we knew we'd just created a legendary family story.

Deer & Deer Hunting
December 2003

Not Enough Chances

2008 was the year that really got me fired up about deer hunting in Minnesota. I saw more rutting activity that year than I've ever seen, before or since.

It was my third season hunting the Gopher State. I actually saw several does and fawns during the three days I hunted in 2006 and shot a forkhorn in 2007. But in 2008, I did some scouting and found a new spot that looked promising. I had no idea just how good it would be.

I planned to camp the night before season so I wouldn't have a long drive in the morning. I was the only one staying at the campground. There were dozens of sites available, but when I pulled into my assigned spot, I found a wide-racked buck tending a doe in my campsite! The deer trotted off, but the buck left a lasting impression in my mind. He was wide and had a lot of points. I didn't get a good look at him, but if I had to guess, just at a glance, I'd say he was a 140-class 10-pointer. Now I was excited!

During my fall scouting, I'd found a ridge with a heavy deer trail at the top. Plus, the aspen and birch forest was relatively open, so I'd have a good vantage point if deer moved downhill from me. I have mixed feelings about entering the woods the day before season. I don't like to contaminate the area with human scent, but I decided I'd rather put my climbing stand at the base of my tree now, rather than fight through the woods with a climber on my back in the dark.

I grabbed the climber, walked about 100 yards and a different buck trotted across the trail, nose to the ground, looking for a doe. The seeking phase of the rut was peaking at just the right time!

I scrapped my plan of leaving the climber in the woods and headed back to the truck. Optimism surged through me and it was tough to repress my excitement for opening morning and get some sleep that night.

To my disappointment, I awoke opening morning to 20 mph winds. It was not ideal weather, but when it's opening day, you hunt.

When I'm hunting a spot on public ground for the first time, I always tiptoe lightly. I know how it feels to have "some idiot" come waltzing through your spot just at first light on opening day. It's frustrating and I've had hunters do that to me on numerous occasions. So when the shoe is on the other foot, I'm always mindful of other hunters.

I was pleased to find no one hunting in the immediate area as I scaled a birch with my climber. However, the relief I felt in having the spot to myself was drowned out by the anxiety of sitting in a tree in gusty winds. Well, if deer weren't supposed to move in the wind, no one told them. By noon I'd seen eight deer. Unfortunately, most of them were crossing downhill of me; not on the ridge where I expected them to be. At noon I climbed down and moved 100 yards downhill, where the deer were crossing.

I climbed into a wide birch tree, facing straight downhill. Not long after repositioning, a single doe came by. She crossed close to me and gave me a good look. It looked like the move was paying off.

All was quiet then until about a half-hour before dark. That's when I heard a grunt downhill and to my left. I snapped my head in the direction of the sound. Seconds later, a deer materialized from behind some cedars. And that's when I made a mistake that has haunted me to this day. I shouldered my rifle, looked through the scope and saw that it was a doe. But I'd heard a grunt, and only bucks make that sound. In hindsight, if I could go back, I would have immediately turned my attention toward the cedars to see what was following her.

But I didn't. Instead, I stayed focused on the doe. She entered the relatively open area and began walking from my left to my right. I was too focused on her and didn't see the next deer until he had crossed an open area that likely would have given me a shot, or at least a good look at him.

The second deer stopped with its shoulder in the wide open, about 65 yards away. But its head was behind a tree.

"Shoot!" my gut screamed. I knew I was looking at a big-bodied deer. And only bucks grunt. Even if I was wrong, my tag was good for any deer.

But the rational side of me told me I needed to see what was on the deer's head and I held fire.

The deer stood exposed, tempting me, for a few seconds. Then it lowered its head from behind the tree that had screened it and swept forward. I didn't need to look twice! It was the big buck that was in my campsite the day before!

Before I could shoot, the buck was behind some brush again. His lady friend, however, was in the open. It was just a matter of time.

The buck moved again but was making a career of screening itself behind brush, deadfalls and trees. I could have shot the doe over and over. But I never got a look at anything more than an ear or a leg on the buck.

The doe led him across the hill below me. Always he remained behind something. The doe stopped now and the buck stayed with her just a few feet away. Here he was, the biggest buck I'd ever seen with a rifle in my hands, only 50 yards away, but I couldn't shoot.

The doe bedded down now, in no hurry to leave. That would have been just fine, except, the sun was rapidly sinking in the west. I was running out of time! I had to try something. I grunted to make the buck think a rival deer was approaching, but the sound didn't even faze him.

"Come on!" I pleaded. "Move!"

But the buck was content to remain with his lover.

I now had only two minutes to shoot. In desperation, I rattled. Still nothing.

The seconds ticked by. I sat 50 yards from my best buck ever, completely powerless to do anything. Darkness fell. The clock had run out. As I descended the tree with my climber, the deer simply walked off.

I walked back to my truck that night feeling utterly deflated.

On the second morning, I relocated to a new tree just a few yards away from the one I'd sat in the previous evening. If deer crossed where the buck and doe were the night before, I'd be far enough over the lip of the hill to get a shot. To this day, the waypoint for that tree is in my GPS as "Day 2 Stand."

Well, against all odds, I'd seen that buck two days in a row. What were the chances I'd see him again? Hunting the big woods isn't like hunting in farm country. For one thing, I've never used trail cameras there. Although there are trails, most of the deer movement seems to be random. And deer densities are low enough that it might be days before a buck passes through an area again. I don't often see the same buck twice when I'm hunting.

On Day 2, I actually saw a respectable 9-pointer. I had him dead to rights, walking broadside in the open. Any other year I'd have shot him. But with the memory of that monster fresh in my mind, I held off on the slim hope that I'd get another crack at him. The 9-pointer with the crab claw on his left antler got a free pass and I watched him for several minutes before he finally disappeared.

On the third day, a pair of hunters decided to do a deer drive through the cedar swamp that began just a short rifle shot to my right. They walked right by me and disappeared into the swamp. A while later they emerged from the swamp, staggered 50 yards apart.

I wasn't amused that people would do a drive with me right in the middle. But I got the last laugh. An hour after they completed the push, a spike buck came out of the swamp they'd just walked through and crossed 15 yards from me.

While I hunted, I'd been texting my friends to see how they were faring. My friend Andy was intrigued by all the bucks I'd seen and I invited him to come hunt with me. He had Veteran's Day off, which was the fourth day of the season, so he asked to take off the third day as well.

That afternoon, I led him to the ridge I'd hunted on opening day. He decided to hunt farther down the ridge from where I'd sat opening morning so we wouldn't be so close together.

That evening, a fox trotted past me. Fur prices were pretty good that year and I'd lost my job. Although I didn't shoot, after the fox left, I was kind of kicking myself. I vowed if I saw it again I'd shoot, knowing full well I probably wouldn't. Ten minutes later it returned. What was I to do? I shot it.

I met Andy back at our trucks that evening. He had carried his climber out, which was notable because it was steel, rather than aluminum and was ridiculously heavy. He had planned to hunt that evening and the following morning, so I was surprised to see that he'd brought his stand out of the woods.

Well, shooting that fox had messed everything up. Andy heard me shoot and figured I had a deer down and would need help. For some reason, that meant he should carry his stand out and we were done hunting.

That night, we slept in the topper of my truck. The fox, which I had put back there, reeked. We came to our senses and put the dead fox in the back of Andy's open pickup bed for the night.

The following morning, the plan was to hunt until noon. I didn't see a thing all morning, so at 11:50, I was on the ground, trimming a few branches that I thought could possibly obstruct a shot toward the uphill side of my tree. That's when a rifle cracked in Andy's direction. I hustled to him, excited to see his deer.

When I walked up to him, however, he wasn't excited. In fact, he seemed nervous.

"Nice buck!" I said, slapping him on the back. But he wasn't excited.

"Is this the one you passed up the other day?" he asked. "He's got a crab claw on the left side."

After a quick look, I was sure it was the same deer.

"Sorry," he said, hanging his head.

My friend Andy shot this buck after he had climbed out of his tree to head home. I'd seen this buck a few days earlier and ordinarily would have shot him, except I'd seen a much bigger buck and was hoping to get a crack at that one.

"Is that what this is about? I didn't pass him up because I thought he needed to grow; I passed him up because I knew there was a bigger one around!"

I wasn't mad at all. In fact, I was thrilled for Andy. It was his biggest buck at the time.

As we dragged Andy's buck back to our trucks – along with that ridiculously heavy deer stand – Andy told me how it went. He had just climbed down from his tree when the buck chased a doe right in front of him. Andy grabbed his rifle and shot the buck, which was staring at him from only 30 yards away. Talk about timing!

We took some pictures of Andy's deer near the truck. Although it had a narrow rack, the deer had a big body! We loaded the deer in Andy's truck and began driving. We hadn't even driven a quarter-mile before the wide-racked monster crossed right in front of us, taunting us!

"See, that's why I passed up your buck," I remarked.

I hunted the next three days in a row, but I never saw that buck again.

All for a Doe

The final morning of the late antlerless season dawned nothing like I'd expected. Nine inches of powdery snow had fallen overnight, blanketing my truck and making the roads a marshmallowy mess.

It had been an incredible season. I'd already killed four deer. I really didn't need to go deer hunting, especially since I was planning to give the deer away if I shot one.

It would have been easy enough to pull up the covers and wallow in my warm cocoon, content to know I'd had a good season.

But the fact that it was the final day of deer season needled me. I felt guilty, in fact, that I was squandering an opportunity. We wait for deer season all year, and now I was about to give up before it was over? It was just a little snow.

It wasn't the prospect of more venison that finally drove me from my cozy bed. Rather, it was the chance to explore some new country. I'd moved to the area two years earlier and had barely scratched the surface of a large tract of public land I'd been hunting. I'd killed a couple does there earlier in the season; in fact, one of them I'd shot with a muzzleloader a few days earlier and it was currently hanging in my friend Jon's garage. I was supposed to help him butcher it that afternoon.

But I had some time to hunt. Between the guilt of missing the final day and the excitement of exploring some new ground, I laced up my boots.

As I exited the truck, I learned the snow wasn't the only thing I had to contend with. A blast of arctic air engulfed me the moment I opened the truck door, and the icy wind ripped my breath away. My nose wrinkled and I gasped to catch my breath. So relentless was the wind that I had to walk backwards across an open area just to breathe.

My legs post-holed through the deep snow, and progress was measured one small step at a time. I felt helpless and weak; an unfit predator in the extreme elements.

Minutes passed as I fought through the snow and wind for the protection of the woods. My lungs struggled for air in the open expanse, but the worst was yet to come. A steep hill stood as the final barrier between me and the sheltering trees. I foundered up the hill, sinking beyond my knees in the drifts, yearning for breath, all while trying not to stumble and bury my rifle in the fluffy powder. I summited the meager hill with all the gusto of someone who has just reached the top of Mt. Everest, but there was no time for celebration. This was just Phase 1. The real game was about to begin.

Although I was there under the guise of deer hunting, the real plan was to explore the aspen-covered hills. Up to this point, I'd only gotten a superficial look at the area, but I liked what I saw. There was plenty of room to roam and my GPS was in my pocket. I just needed to find my way back by late afternoon to help Jon butcher that deer. With that barebones plan in mind, I was free to explore. I pointed my nose into the wind and set out.

Progress in the knee-deep snow was slow, but there was no need to hurry. In fact, my steps in the fluffy snow were whisper quiet, and with the wind in my face, it was actually conceivable that I could come upon a deer, although I didn't hold high hopes. I was perfectly content just to explore.

I hadn't even been walking for a half-hour before I came across a set of deer tracks cutting a clean path through the snow. The storm had subsided only that morning and there wasn't a flake in the tracks. They were ultra-fresh; wind hadn't even sifted fine grains of snow into them. I pondered how long it might take to catch up to a deer, given the deep snow, even though I knew the tracks couldn't have been more than an hour old.

I plodded along, rifle ready to snap to my shoulder at a moment's notice. Although my movements were laborious in the snow, they were at least quiet.

I was stunned, actually, when after only 200 yards of ridiculously easy tracking, I spotted a brown form that looked out of place, not 30 yards away. The deer was facing away with its head down and had no idea I was sidling up behind it.

I shouldered my rifle, peered through the scope and waited for the deer to raise its head. Only antlerless deer were legal, and I needed to make sure I wasn't looking at a buck.

It was only moments before the doe raised its head. I didn't have a good shot at the body, with the doe's posterior pointed toward me, but I reasoned at 30 yards I could take a head shot and my hunt would be over quickly. But to my surprise, when I fired, the deer bolted.

I watched incredulously as the deer bounded away through the snow. How had I missed a chip shot? I couldn't imagine what went wrong. I felt steady. It should have been a done deal.

The jig was up now. The doe, which had been oblivious to the predator on her backtrail, had gotten a fast education. I gave her a few minutes to settle down, then I took up her track for another crack at her. With all the snow, she couldn't hide; it was just a matter of whether I could catch up to a now-wary deer.

I trailed the doe's bounding tracks roughly back in the direction from which I'd came. I slogged down the hill in the deep snow, feeling like a bulky child swaddling in an excessive amount of winter clothing by an overprotective mother. I could move only with difficulty, while the doe had easily put distance between us. I felt unfit as a predator.

Luckily, by the time I'd crested the next hill, the doe's pace had slowed to a walk. No doubt she glanced at her backtrail as she reached the next hill to watch the bumbling orange pumpkin coming after her.

I appreciated her slower pace. I didn't want to run a marathon. Besides, I needed to get to Jon's in the afternoon to help him with the doe I'd already shot days earlier. There was a good chance this chase would end when the clock ran out and not when I caught up to the deer.

The tracks meandered here and there atop the hill, and soon, the doe joined up with at least one other deer. Would a second set of eyes make it harder for me to sneak up on the deer, or would a companion distract her? I didn't know what to expect.

As I followed the tracks, I couldn't help but dwell on the fact that I'd missed such an easy shot. Granted, it was a free-handed shot, but at 30 yards, I thought I should have dropped her where she stood. It was a clean miss, at least. There was no blood or hair where she'd been standing, nor anywhere along the trail.

Soon, my doe joined up with more deer. I half expected she was gathering an enraged harem to attack me. Now there was no telling which was the original track. It didn't matter. The first bald-headed deer that gave me a shot would be my target.

I might ordinarily have gotten cold on a single-digit day, but the exertion of picking up one foot out of the knee-deep snow and shoving it forward again forced me to unzip my jacket. Hot breath coated my beard and mustache with water vapor, which froze into ever-lengthening icicles. Sweat billowed out of me. I had no choice but to trudge forward. Sweaty as I was, if I stopped for more than a minute or two, the perspiration trickling down my body would surely chill me to the core.

Up ahead, a herd of deer I had not yet seen high-stepped it through the snow. Behind them, their pursuer plodded along. How far ahead were they? A hundred yards? A half-mile? I had no way of knowing. Perhaps they were staying just ahead of me, keeping constant tabs on their assailant.

This tracking job was just what I needed. I had set out that morning more to explore the area than to shoot a deer, and this little deer herd was giving me a grand tour. It's a wonderful feeling to know you have the freedom to roam wherever you like and at the end of the day, the GPS in your pocket will get you home.

Like a grouse hunter, I remained tightly wound, ready to snap the gun up in an instant. The deer could be a mile away or just around the next bend. I had to be ready. Odds are I wouldn't be afforded a lot of time to shoot and if I busted the deer, no doubt the chase would be extended for at least another hour. The responsible side of me reminded myself I needed to make good on an opportunity so I could get to Jon's. But my body was more concerned with saving myself the added exertion of another extension to the chase.

I had lost count of how many hills the deer had led me up and over. Maybe they were trying to wear me down. But as I crested yet another rise, suddenly, there they were! Brown stood out everywhere against the snowy backdrop. Four, five, maybe more deer stared back at me, seemingly as surprised to see me as I was to see them. The exact number didn't matter; I needed to pick out the doe that afforded me the best shot. I swung onto a doe, standing broadside about 50 yards away and squeezed the trigger. The rifle blast reverberated across the snow-deadened landscape and sent deer scurrying everywhere. But the one I'd shot at was down, although it was struggling to regain its feet. I hustled forward, rifle at the ready. She was far livelier than she should have been, and when I was just a few yards away, I put a finishing shot in her.

As I approached her, I saw that my first shot hit her in the back leg. Now I was really perplexed. Later, at the rifle range, it all became clear: my scope was way off, and in fact, was broken. Even when I adjusted the windage, the crosshairs no longer moved. I thought back to an incident a week earlier when I bent down to move a log with a climbing tree stand on my back. As I bent, the stand slipped off one shoulder and hit the rifle hard. That had to be what had caused the scope to be off. It was a shame. I hate to wound deer, but I'm thankful I was able to dispatch the doe quickly. It also explains how I had missed the first shot completely.

It was now midday and although the chase was over, the real work was

A sled helped me whisk this hard-earned doe right over 9 inches of new snow.

just beginning. I decided the sled in my truck would make dragging the deer easier over the deep snow. The pursuit had taken me more or less in the direction of my truck, which was a deciding factor in the decision to get the sled. I marked the doe on the GPS and retrieved the sled.

Once I'd retrieved the sled from my truck and made it back to the doe, I called Jon.

"Hey, are you still planning to butcher that deer today?" I asked, feigning a sleepy voice.

"Yeah," he responded. "You're still coming over to help me, right?"

"I don't know. I'm still in bed," I lied.

"Seriously?"

"No," I laughed. "Actually, I just shot another one."

"Seriously?" he repeated

"Yup."

"What time will you be over?"

"Well, as soon as I can get her out of the woods."

The doe's entrails warmed my hands as I gutted her. It was a bit of a challenge in the fluffy snow. I had to pack down snow to create a flat area to work. With that job finished, I rolled her into my sled. I soon learned that taking the time to slog back for the sled had been a wise move. The

A relentless wind, coupled with single-digit temperatures caused my breath to freeze and form beard-sicles.

sled floated over the snow and pulling the deer was almost effortless. Plus, I now had tracks to step in.

Even though the deer pulled like a dream, it was still work. And even though it was downhill to the truck, gravity can be too much of a good thing. At times I had to spin the sled around and let the doe down in a somewhat slow, controlled manner ahead of me. The worst part was in the final push toward the truck. Back out in the open, the wind was howling. It drifted over my old tracks and purloined my breath. Again, I had to walk backwards at times just to breathe.

Slowly, steadily the truck loomed nearer. At long last, I reached the vehicle and dropped the tailgate. With great exertion, I hoisted the doe into the bed of the truck. Then I slouched into the driver's seat and made for Jon's.

As we turned carcasses to meat, I relayed the tale of my hunt. Jon shook his head.

"And all for a doe," he said.

A Tale of Two Whitetails

It was the best of times, it was the worst of times. It was a buck with wisdom, it was a buck with foolishness. And it was two stories of incredulity, not just one.

That little tip of my blaze-orange cap to Charles Dickens could summarize one particular deer hunt I experienced on a Minnesota deer hunt.

It was late in the rifle season, and as usual, I still had my buck tag. Opening weekend had come and gone without much action. I'd tried some new spots; tried some new things, but I didn't have a thing to show for it. It was time to get serious.

I tried a new spot I'd had my eye on for a while. It was sort of a broad funnel and I know bucks travel through it as they search for estrous does.

On Wednesday, the 12th day of the season, I gave it a sit. I saw a doe and a fawn that morning, but that was it. It was odd, I thought, that the fawn was in the lead. They approached to within 10 yards and I watched them for close to an hour, with snot running down to my chin, but I was unable to move, lest I scare them. I was almost relieved when they finally wandered off. I hoped that mom would attract a suitor, but such was not the case.

The next morning, the 13th day, I again hunted the same spot. I felt pretty good about the location. Once again, the doe and fawn appeared, with the fawn leading the way. This time they crossed on the opposite side of me and didn't loiter nearly as long. After they passed, I stood in my climbing stand and turned to face behind me – the direction they had come from – to see if anything with antlers might be trailing them.

About 20 minutes had passed since I'd seen the doe and fawn, but I remained standing, whether through sheer optimism or just because it felt good to stretch. Suddenly, I heard the unmistakable sound of a twig snapping in the crisp, frosty air. Could it be a buck on the doe's trail? I strained to see through a copse of brush.

Sure enough, there was a deer coming, all right, and it was a buck! It was the first one I'd seen all season, and with only one more day to hunt before the Wisconsin opener, I was ready to shoot!

Soon, the buck was about 30 yards away. He was partially veiled by brush, but at that distance, the bullet would have no trouble reaching him, I reasoned. Still, if I just let him keep coming, he would give me a wide-open shot. I had every reason to believe he would follow the same tack taken by the doe and fawn 20 minutes earlier.

It was a gamble. Waiting like that is the sort of decision that can come back to bite you, but he did exactly as I hoped. Now, instead of a 30-yard shot through the brush, I had a 50-yard broadside shot with nary a twig between us.

I shouldered the .270, found the buck in the scope and squeezed the trigger. A loud metallic "click!" reverberated through the 0-degree air. The buck snapped his head up and looked straight at me. I froze with the rifle still pointed at him.

It took me about a half-second to figure out what had happened. I have developed a habit of sticking the magazine in my rifle when I use my climbing stand. I don't load a round in the chamber for safety. Then, after I've reached my hunting height and settled in, I simply work the action to load the rifle. It's safe and there's no way I can possibly drop the magazine and need to climb down to retrieve it. But now, for the first time ever, I'd forgotten to pump a round into the chamber.

The buck and I were now engaged in a chess match and it was his move. He stared in my direction, and all I could do was try to hold still. Luckily, he didn't seem too perturbed by the incident, and after just a few seconds, he resumed his lope for love.

Shuck, shuck! The sound of me pumping the .270 was much louder than the click of the firing pin finding no primer. The buck halted again as if to say, "I *knew* I heard something!" but before he could finish his thought, I'd sent 130 grains of lead right at his heart. He bounded off and crashed through a fallen cedar tree a short distance away.

He was a Joe Shead buck if I ever saw one. The 2-1/2-year-old buck sported 8 spindly points, none of them longer than 4 inches. Half of those were chipped or broken. For some unknown reason his forehead was covered in ice, and he was so rutty, he smelled almost like gasoline. Well, just the same, I was happy to have him.

I returned to my climber and packed the stand and my rifle out to the truck. I then returned for the buck.

I called a buddy and was telling him about my morning conquest as I returned to retrieve my deer. It was an easy walk down the trail and it wasn't hard to carry on a phone conversation. I reached the point where I

Not only was this buck just plain dumb; he sported a meager rack and had broken 4 of his 8 points. He was a Joe Shead buck if there ever was one! Had he been smarter and ran when I pulled the trigger with an empty chamber, I might have still been in my stand a half-hour later when a much bigger buck appeared.

needed to cut into the woods, now only about 120 yards from where I had been hunting. Suddenly, motion caught my eye!

"You're not going to believe this!" I whispered into the phone. "There's a big buck walking right at me!"

A buck – much larger than the one I had just shot – was 25 yards away and walking closer, despite the fact that I was talking on the phone! I can't be sure, but I think he may have mistaken the sound of me walking for that of another deer.

The buck stopped and looked at me, completely unconcerned. His body was relaxed. His ears didn't stand erect. Everything about him gave the impression he hadn't a care in the world.

Our eyes locked on each other. Because he was facing head-on, I couldn't tell you how many points he carried, but the thing that's etched in my mind is the length of his brow tines. They were as tall as his G-2s!

We stood looking at each other for several seconds. Finally, he just turned and slowly walked away.

That's when hindsight entered into the picture. Any other time you let a deer walk a little closer, something usually goes wrong. But when I waited for my buck to clear the brush, he did exactly like I hoped. If my buck had any sense of intelligence, he would have run at the clicking firing pin, or at the very least, he should have been on edge from it and then immediately bolted at the sound of the pumping rifle. But he was just too darn dumb, hence, the reason a guy like me was able to tag him. And had he ran off, I'd still have been sitting in my stand – admittedly cursing my bad luck over the blown opportunity, but still sitting there – when the big boy showed up a half-hour later.

I weeded out the dumb genes, which should be passed along for the sake of deer hunters everywhere, and left the smart buck to do the breeding. It ain't that there's no deer out there; they're just getting too darn smart. I take full responsibility for that.

Outdoor News
Nov. 11, 2016

Wisconsin Outdoor News
Nov. 25, 2016

My Biggest Buck

2015 was an awful year for me, but it turned out to be a great deer season.

It had been a rough summer. I was busy at work; too busy. There was too much to do and I was stretched too thin. I wasn't able to take the time to fish or take a good road trip. I said "no" to far too many offers to go fishing that summer or duck hunting in the early fall. A nonstop barrage of flat tires, broken windows and other mini disasters had welled up inside of me. I was cranky and in sore need of something to go my way.

Oh, and then there was the house. Just a year earlier, I had purchased my first home. It was a fixer-upper and needed a lot more work than I expected. Taking care of the obvious things wasn't too bad. We added insulation, new plumbing, a new furnace and a new water heater. Then there were the hidden surprises – like the fact that there was a rotten section of my living room wall where the roof was leaking. Fixing that was going to be a major undertaking!

My brother offered a hand, but couldn't come until November – opening day of deer season to be exact. So I had one morning to hunt. My brother and I spent the next eight days putting in a new wall, from the foundation right up to the roof. It wasn't how I wanted to spend my deer season!

On Day 10, I was exhausted, but the wall project was behind me. I could finally get back to deer hunting. I awoke to strong winds and damp, cold air. Rain was in the forecast. I thought about not hunting. It was going to be ugly. But what was I thinking? Not going hunting today would be crazy! All week I'd longed to hunt, and now I was considering not going? Besides, the weather could work to my advantage. I quickly assembled hunting gear and hopped in the truck. I looked at the sky as if to say, "Bring it on!"

I didn't see many deer on the drive that morning. Over the years, the number of deer I see on that drive has proven to be a somewhat reliable indicator of the number of deer I see while hunting. The deer are either moving or they're not. No matter. I was craving a chance to salvage my season. Although it was windy, the rain wasn't forecast to start until 10:00.

I reached my hunting area and shinnied up a tree. The wind wasn't so bad in the shelter of the woods and it actually didn't seem like a bad morning to hunt. But the limited deer sightings on my drive proved to be an accurate forecast of the morning deer activity. I didn't see a single deer from my tree. At 9:45 a.m., the rain started, just as the weatherman predicted. It was time to implement Phase 2.

I didn't want to sit in the rain, although I didn't really mind hiking in a light rain. With wind to mask my footsteps and wet leaves to deaden them, I figured I could move through the woods pretty stealthily. My plan was to take a long walk and still-hunt my way back to my truck. After a summer of bad luck, followed up by more than a week of nothing but house projects, I needed a good walk to clear my head anyway. But to be honest, I'd already proven the deer weren't moving, so still-hunting was probably my best option to shoot a deer anyway.

I quietly slipped out of my stand and walked downwind along a power line cut for a good mile. The plan was to still-hunt into the wind back to my truck, and I didn't care if it took me all day. When I was satisfied with the distance to cover, I cut into the woods near some cedar trees. Immediately my mind went into shed hunting mode. It looked like an ideal place to find an antler. "No, you idiot! You're supposed to be deer hunting!" I chastised myself. Those cedars gave way to more cedars. It looked like a phenomenal wintering area, and soon, I was just shed hunting. "All right." I allowed. "I'll look under these few trees, but that's it!"

I came up empty, which was just as well. I didn't need to carry an antler while I tried to sneak through the woods.

Now I had to train my eyes to look 3 feet off the ground instead of scanning the forest floor. It's funny, I get used to looking at the ground because I shed hunt so much and I consciously have to remind my eyes to look higher when I get into deer season.

I began picking my way through the mixed stand of aspen, birch and cedars. Thanks to the wind and light rain, I was able to move deathly quietly.

It's hard enough to sneak up on deer undetected, but here, the woods were fairly open, so I moved painfully slowly as I picked apart the landscape in an attempt to see deer before they saw me. The fact deer could easily see me was my Achilles heel. But the odds were pretty good that they wouldn't smell or hear me, given the rain and wind. Slowly, cautiously I moved ahead, taking just a few steps and then scanning diligently, trying to pick out something that just didn't look right – a flicking tail, a white throat patch or a horizontal line of a deer's back in a vertical world. I paused behind trees when I could, using them to break up my outline and also serving as a rest, should I need to take a shot. It felt good to be walking through the woods again. It was just what my head needed.

I had only been creeping along for maybe 20 minutes when movement ahead grabbed my attention. I froze. Hooves thumped the ground and a flash of brown appeared through the trees. In moments, I spotted a doe trotting through the woods, coming right at me. As luck would have it, I had paused right behind a cedar tree, which served as great screening cover. With a quick peek through the scope, I confirmed it was a doe. She paused for a moment and looked behind her. My gaze immediately followed hers, and seconds later, another deer appeared. I didn't need to look through my scope to know this was a buck! The buck cruised along, nose to the ground, clearly in pursuit of the doe. The doe was playing hard to get and she trotted off as the buck drew near. In seconds, she had drawn parallel with me about 50 yards to the side. Every indication was that the buck would follow in her tracks and give me a chip shot.

My heart hammered in my chest. I completely had the drop on these deer. What's more, this buck was one of the biggest I have ever seen while hunting. I couldn't believe I was actually going to get a shot at him!

The doe passed me without any indication that she knew I was there. If all went well, the buck would follow right behind her, giving me a broadside shot. All I had to do was let him stroll right into my trap. About that time, the doe starting to put a little distance on him. The buck, which up until this point had been moving along at a brisk walk, decided he needed to catch up and he broke into a dead run. "No!" I thought. Here he was, my dream buck, just 50 yards away, but running so fast through the trees there was no way I could get a shot. I wouldn't even know how to aim at a target moving that fast.

My mind spun like a slot machine reel and the thought that spun to the surface was of a 9-year-old boy hunting with his father for the first time. My dad had given me a small whistle that I was to blow if we saw a running buck. The idea was the deer would stop at the sound and give Dad a standing shot. I'd never gotten a chance to try it, but in one of those time-stands-still moments, the idea flooded into my mind.

I did the only thing I could do. "Hey!" I yelled at the bounding buck. The buck slammed on the brakes 50 yards away, now broadside to me. He

My rifle roared and the biggest buck I'd ever shot at disappeared. For a moment I kicked myself. I had rushed the shot! Why hadn't I taken another split-second to settle the cross-hairs? Luckily, my shot was true and I found the buck piled up only 30 yards away. Talk about relief!

obviously was looking at the source of the sound now, and I knew I didn't have much time to shoot. I quickly lined up the cross-hairs behind his front shoulder and touched the trigger. The explosion rocked the woods and the buck turned and fled on the doe's backtrail.

The smell of burnt gunpowder hung heavy in the damp November air. The reverberations of the rifle's roar died out, then everything was silent. The buck was gone.

"No!" I thought. I'd blown it. The buck was supposed to drop right there, but he was gone. In my haste to shoot, I'd rushed it. I should've settled the cross-hairs for just another half a beat. I was afraid, at best, I'd gotten a bad hit and the rain would quickly wash away any blood trail. I raced to the spot where the buck had been standing just seconds ago, then stumbled off in the direction he had gone, mentally kicking myself for rushing the shot the whole time. Why, oh why, hadn't I just taken another moment to settle the cross-hairs? I had the time. It was a chip shot at a great buck and I rushed it.

My stomach was in knots and I muttered under my breath. But a brown patch of fur on the ground erased my anguish. There he was, stone dead,

On a rainy, windy day, I used the weather to my advantage to slip quietly through the woods. Although I was soaked, tagging my best buck ever after a frustrating year was a sweet reward.

only 30 yards from where he'd been standing when I shot.

Immediately, a weight lifted off my chest. The buck was mine. It was more than just a deer or a best buck. It was a reward for a lousy summer and a house project that cheated me out of my deer season. I don't know if I deserved that buck or if I earned it or if it was just karma intervening, but none of that matters. All I know is shooting that 10-pointer took a heck of a lot of the sting out of my lousy 2015.

Sweetness

The 2019 Minnesota deer season was a quiet one. I didn't see many deer in the woods or even on the back of pickup trucks. I hunted eight mornings, but in all those sits I saw just a small 6-pointer and a doe. I'd moved to different areas, heck, even different counties, but I just wasn't seeing deer. I needed a change even more radical than just trying different stand sites.

On Thursday, the 13th day of the season, it came.

Overnight, snow fell in the Arrowhead region. I slept in that morning and left the climber at home. My plan was to put an ancient technique into action: I'd cut a track in the new-fallen snow and follow it. You could sit in a tree for hours, never knowing if you'd see a deer or not. But at the end of every deer track is a deer. And that was encouragement enough for me.

My destination was a large parcel of public land that would give me room to roam and let me follow the tracks wherever they led. I specifically chose this place because of its vastness and because of its conifer cover, which would give deer shelter during a snowstorm.

Within 10 minutes of leaving the truck, I'd cut a track in the fresh snow. The track was large, but I'm not skilled enough to tell a buck track from a doe. Still, it seemed promising.

The tracks were easy to follow where there was fresh snow, but under the canopy of large conifers there was bare ground or at best, a flexible sheet of ice from the freezing rain that had preceded the snow. On this flexible ice, I hardly left tracks myself and the difficulty of tracking increased. I did the best I could and circled to snowier areas if I lost the track. Doing this, I was able to follow the deer.

Tracking this deer revealed its daily activities much more than you'd see just from watching a deer walk past your stand. The deer was constantly on the move; never stopping to feed or bed down. This made me think I was following a buck that was on the hunt for does. I decided he had to have a name, but the first name that popped into my head was Ralph, which seemed like a dumb name for a deer. Soon after I named him, he cut through an open area where tall grass had been coated with ice and had bent over somewhat. He sort of high-stepped through this area, which reminded me of the way Walter Payton used to high-step on the football field, so I immediately changed the deer's name to Sweetness – Payton's nickname. I liked that much better.

It wasn't long before Sweetness encountered another deer. Suddenly, this predictable line of tracks began circling like a cyclone. Round and round the deer ran and it seemed apparent that indeed Sweetness was a buck and he was trying to court a doe. Following these tracks running around willy-nilly was enough to make a guy dizzy. Finally, I grew tired of the horsing around and I made a wide circle in an effort to pick up the tracks again when they continued in a more meaningful direction. It took me a while to unravel it, but finally the pair ambled off to the left after they were done running around.

Only a few minutes after I left the cyclone area, I jumped them. They were 50 yards ahead. I couldn't see antlers, but the smaller deer ran left while the larger one went right. I assumed this was a buck and a doe and that Sweetness would soon come looking for his lady, so I froze for 5 minutes, waiting for him to come back. But he never returned.

I took up the larger deer's tracks where I'd last seen him fleeing. There were other deer tracks on the slight hill where he'd disappeared, but I knew I was looking for the wide-spaced tracks of a running deer. The distance between them made finding them tricky, but I knew which direction he was heading and I finally cut a few good tracks before he got under the conifers and went across a sheet of that icy ground.

Back in the snow, the tracks were unmistakable. They were obviously only minutes old and they were deep and fresh, with distinct dewclaws. In places where he was still hurrying, he even kicked up a little dirt.

From reading legendary tracker Larry Benoit's book, *How to Bag the Biggest Buck of Your Life*, I figured the buck would try to put some distance between us before slowing down, so for a while, I moved quickly. But as I got back into the conifers, I slowed my pace to a stealthy creep. I tried to keep my eyes up, looking for deer as much as possible and just glancing at the track as needed. Of course, there were places where the tracks required my full attention to decipher. I spent a lot of time hunched over, trying to see under the conifers if a buck was up ahead, looking back at his pursuer.

Another set of deer tracks intersected Sweetness' and it threw me for a loop. Soon after the other deer's tracks crossed, Sweetness' tracks led

Sweetness' tracks were only minutes old. They were sharp and crisp in the fresh snow and at times, he kicked up snow and dirt as he hustled through the woods in his search for does. These tracks, however, were his undoing.

through another icy area and I struggled to find hoof prints. I circled back to where I had good tracks and went left and right. I circled around so many times in that spot that I couldn't tell which tracks were my original set and which direction I had been heading. After a few anxious minutes, I finally got back on my original tracks, circled ahead and found the deer tracks that I'd lost.

Tracking a deer seems easy in theory. You follow the tracks and eventually you find the deer. But it's humbling to see how easily simply crossing another track or going through an area with no snow can throw you. My hat is off to those woodsmen who can routinely track deer, especially when the snow is a few days old and other deer have tracked up the landscape.

Finally, I was back on track, literally. Now, Sweetness disappeared into a stand of mature balsams – the kind of trees that contain a million dead, dry branches near the ground that snap with the slightest touch. Luckily, the weather was on my side. In addition to the new snow, it was windy. Trees swayed, groaned and creaked in the blow. During gusts, I'd pick up the pace and when the wind died down, I slowed down or stopped altogether. Mother Nature was giving me every advantage. I just needed a little luck.

I popped out of the balsams into a more open area of woods, quite relieved to be out of the twig-snapping gauntlet. I gazed into the clearing, and there was a buck! He was walking slowly, quartering toward me only 20 yards away! I'd already decided that if Sweetness was a buck – any buck – I was going to shoot. What a feat to track down a buck on his own turf!

The buck was oblivious to the guy in orange standing mere feet away. He was walking along, distracted by some more deer tracks just outside the conifers.

I raised my gun, but before I could shoot, he stepped behind two trees, so I had to let him keep walking toward me, just hoping that he wouldn't see or smell me before I could shoot.

In seconds, he cleared the trees and I fired when he was 18 steps away. He never even knew I was there.

As I skidded the buck through the snowy woods, I reflected on the hunt. To be able to roam a large tract of land open to everyone; to have the freedom to just take up a track and go where it leads you; to spend a day outside breathing clean air in a picturesque forest filled with woodpeckers,

As I emerged from the balsams and entered a clearing, I spotted Sweetness only 20 yards away, quartering toward me! I waited until he cleared some trees, then fired when he was just 18 paces away! He never knew I was there.

squirrels and chickadees; everything was a blessing, whether there's a deer in the truck at the end of the day or not. Sometimes we just lose sight of that.

Outdoor News
Dec. 6, 2019

Sick for Deer Season

The day before deer season I had promised my friend Joe I would duck hunt with him. However, by Thursday evening I wasn't feeling up to duck hunting. I had a fever, chills and a stuffy nose. But if I cancelled, I knew I would have to look into Joe's sad puppy dog eyes and break his heart, so I kept our appointment.

Friday morning I met Joe at the boat landing well before dawn. I was not looking forward to this. As much as I love duck hunting, I'd have much rather been in bed, nestled in my cozy blankets. Nonetheless, we donned waders, set out our decoys and greeted the dawn: Joe with naïve duck hunter's optimism, and me with a blank stare as I concentrated on breathing through my mouth and contemplated the possibility of leaving early.

The hunt wasn't my finest moment. My ears were plugged, which made it hard to hear duck wings cleaving the sky. My senses felt dull; my movements slow and awkward. When we had birds in range, I just wasn't ready for them.

The hunting wasn't too hot, but the morning was punctuated by Joe's first bufflehead: a gorgeous drake that now adorns his living room. By mid-morning, however, the flight had slowed down and my symptoms worsened. Eventually I slogged to shore and laid down on the high ground.

"Here comes a flock! Do you want to shoot?" Joe asked from a cattail clump a few yards away. I just groaned in reply.

"How about these ones?" Joe asked as another flock circled.

"Ugh!" I moaned.

Eventually Joe took pity on me and called it a morning. Packing up was no fun. There were a lot of decoys to retrieve with cold, wet hands, but the thought of going home and flopping down on my bed was good motivation.

I slept most of the day, exhausted from our early morning exertion, coupled with an overall lack of energy. I didn't know how I was going to go deer hunting in the morning, but it was opening day and I couldn't not go. That afternoon I packed my truck with my hunting gear. Usually

I would drive up north the night before season and spend the night in my truck. However, the idea of sleeping in a cold truck topper did not appeal to me in the least. I voted to sleep in my cozy bed and make a long drive early in the morning.

The following morning I had to wake up extra early to make the 75-mile drive. It was a challenging, uncomfortable ride. At times I got chills and I cranked the heater to full blast. But minutes later I'd be sweating and I'd have to turn on the air conditioner. These hot and cold spells alternated for the duration of the drive. How I was going to spend a morning in a tree stand and shoot a deer was beyond me. I hoped a dumb buck would just stumble out right away and I could get the hunt over with.

I shouldered my climbing tree stand, toted my rifle and made the long trek to my stand site. The exertion took my breath away and I stopped frequently. I started the hike with my jacket in hand, but by the time I was halfway to my stand, almost all my upper layers were off. By the time I settled in my tree I was completely exhausted. It would feel good to just sit and rest. I hoped maybe the fresh air would do me good.

I sat, 15 feet up a birch tree, breathing through my mouth and trying not to cough. Maybe I'd get lucky and shoot one right away, but I knew that wasn't likely. I rarely shoot a buck opening morning. I watched the sunrise and began the task of sweeping my eyes back and forth, scanning for any sign of movement.

Usually that opening morning excitement keeps me fired up for several hours. That energy keeps me from snacking or getting distracted by my phone. But for whatever reason that morning, I reached into my pack and pulled out a package of Pop-Tarts.

So there I was, trying to unwrap a foil wrapper silently in the woods – an impossible task. I don't even know why I was eating because the season was only a half-hour old. I was chewing on a Pop-Tart when suddenly a doe came from behind me at a trot. Right on her tail was a buck. I threw the remaining portion of the Pop-Tart into my pack and snapped my rifle to my shoulder. I gave the rack a quick glance and saw that the buck was plenty good enough for me. That buck should have lived to see another day. All he had to do was keep tailing the doe. But for some reason he stopped just before he disappeared behind some trees. He was right in the open and the one branch that could have concealed him was about 6 inches too high to save his life. I snuck a bullet under the branch and the 9-pointer

Shooting this 9-pointer first thing opening morning when I was sick was a big relief. However, by the time I dragged him out of the woods, I decided I needed to extend my hunt.

went down. I couldn't believe it! Here I was, sick as a dog, with a nice buck down on opening morning! What a relief!

I got down from my stand right away. As happy as I was with the buck, I was more relieved that I could go home now. However, I wasn't looking forward to the drag. It would be a fair distance, but at least most of it would be on trails. I tagged and field-dressed the buck, then carried my gun and stand back to my truck, leaving a few layers of clothing behind as well. Then I returned for the deer.

Dragging a deer out of the woods is never particularly fun, but especially when you're sick. At least I didn't have to worry about suppressing my cough now! I took my time, doing the best I could. When I needed to stop, I stopped. I had all day.

But to my delight, my strength was returning. A day earlier and I'd have really struggled getting that deer out of the woods. Today was no picnic by any means, but moving the deer was do-able. Besides, you have to stop now and then to admire your buck's antlers anyway!

By the time I reached the truck, I was actually starting to come around. In fact, although earlier I was excited to go home, now I was embracing the day. My shotgun and a sack of duck decoys were in the back of my truck and there was a nearby lake I had always wanted to hunt … so I decided to go for it!

When I reached the parking spot where I'd have to begin the mile-long hike to the lake, to my surprise, I found a truck already parked there! Who would be duck hunting on opening day of deer season? A minute later I got my answer as a blaze orange-clad hunter exited the woods on the hiking trail. He said he was just hiking along the trail, taking a little midday walk, when he spotted an 8-pointer in the clearing only a couple hundred yards from the truck.

I immediately put my duck hunting plans on hold and offered to help him drag out his buck. It's amazing what a little deer dragging will do for your health!

Was That a Car Door?

The day before deer season, I wrestled my climbing stand though the woods to the tree I had picked a few weeks earlier. I thought it prudent to climb the tree and see if any limbs needed clearing before opening morning. I clanked my way up the tree and looked around. My eyes instantly fell onto a distant ridge. In my mind, angels strummed harps and sang ethereal songs. Just look at that ridge! How could I have missed it?

Even from a quarter-mile away, I knew the ridge was my destiny. The strip of aspens created a natural runway, and I was sure if I sat there, I would kill a buck.

It was an unusual opening morning. I did my due diligence and sat in my pre-selected tree, but all I could think about was that ridge. I decided to stick it out in my opening morning spot until noon before I moved. But I only made it to 11.

At midday, I climbed down and set a course for the ridge. Easier said than done. I had already fought my way along a creek, scampered up a steep hill on hands and knees at times, then bushwhacked through a fortress of trees and brush more impenetrable than Fort Knox. And all while wearing a climbing tree stand on my back. Moving through the woods with that stand was like trying to swim through a net. Every low-hanging branch grabbed the stand and spun me around. And the bungee cord designed to hold the seat back against the trunk snagged every possible vine and bramble, going taut, and at times, snapping back at me. By the time I had made it the half-mile to the original stand site, I was cut up, dripping sweat and reeking so badly any deer that didn't flee at the sound of clanking aluminum had certainly at least winded my stench. In my mind, I envisioned the tree stand manufacturer coming out with its latest model, then going on an expensive hunt to "field test" it. I suspected the hunter walked down a manicured trail leading to a food plot, never passing within 20 feet of a single limb until strapping the stand to a tree. After hunting from the perfectly de-limbed tree and shooting a monster buck, the company declared the stand a success and brought it to market. I was ready to write the company a scathing letter – no, better yet, I'd send them an invite to hunt in some real woods with their new stand! That would teach them!

It was a half-mile from my truck to my opening day tree. And the ridge was another quarter-mile beyond that. After fighting the stand through another quarter-mile of brush and uttering some unmentionable phrases (which also served to scare deer) I finally got set up on the ridge.

My distant vision was correct. It really *did* look promising, and a lot better than my original spot. I don't know how I missed it, but this was before Google Earth, smartphones and the like. The only high-tech equipment I carried was a bare-bones GPS with no background map.

It took me two minutes to scale a birch tree. It took me two hours to stop panting from my arduous struggle with the stand through the woods. A thought finally occurred to me: what if I actually shot a deer? Then I'd *really* have my work cut out for me.

I didn't see a deer that afternoon. I left the stand at the base of the tree overnight. It was still a long hike to my truck in the dark, but at least I didn't have to fight my way through the woods with a stand on my back!

The following morning, I did indeed shoot a buck from atop that ridge. I was excited, of course, but I really dreaded the task of removing the stand and now a buck from the woods. I decided to haul out the stand and my hunting gear first and then come back for the deer.

I sighed, shrugged my shoulders and began the agonizing slog back to my truck, through the brush, through the trees, down a hill that was as bad to go down as it was to go up, and then ultimately uphill along the creek. After finally reaching the truck, I huffed and puffed as I rested on my tailgate, utterly exhausted, but with only one trip complete.

There had to be an easier way! And then my mind replayed a sound I thought I'd heard earlier that morning. As I sat in my tree in the dark, waiting for first light, an unusual sound reached my ears.

"Was that a car door?" I thought.

I decided this sound merited further investigation. Where there are car doors, there are roads. I retrieved an atlas from my truck and took a closer look at the area. Indeed there was a road – a faint, lightly maintained road – about a mile south of where my truck was parked. If that road actually existed, it had to be much closer to where my buck was.

I headed south, and lo and behold I found that little road, which was a scant 200 yards from my buck! I felt like an idiot, for sure, but that slamming car door saved me from one heck of a brutal drag through the woods!

Part II
Camaraderie

The Boltless Dribbler

Andy Lecker is a cop. He's hardworking, honest, loyal; a man of integrity. He's the kind of guy who always has your back. If you forgot something, he's got an extra for you. He's a genuinely good and decent human being.

Which means he's pretty much the polar opposite of me. I'm the guy who forgets things and has to borrow them from Andy. And honesty? I'm willing to bend the truth for a good practical joke.

Andy walks a pretty straight line, but every once in a while, he'll crack a joke. I have a lot of cop friends. None of their jokes are funny.

Anyway, Andy and I shared a deer camp together for a few years in northwestern Wisconsin out of the home of our friends Ryan and Jen. In the early years, Ryan and Jen rented a house just down the road from a large parcel of public hunting land. Later, they bought a house on 10 acres that abutted that public land.

On one of those hunts, Andy earned himself a nickname; a terrible name that doesn't befit such a genuinely nice guy.

It all started on opening morning of deer season. There were four of us crammed into the basement that Ryan and Jen rented. So just imagine four people stumbling around bleary-eyed at 0 dark 30, trying to get layers on, assemble gear, realize they should use the bathroom one more time, re-dress, etc. Andy did all this opening-morning scrambling while wearing only his long johns. A prudent guy like Andy wouldn't want to run around the house overdressed and get all sweated up. Well, during his early morning visit to the bathroom, he either leaned up against a wet sink, or more likely, didn't quite get the plumbing shut off after he finished draining his bladder. When he emerged from the bathroom, there was a wet spot on the front of his long johns. And everyone noticed.

Some ribbing ensued. True or not, as far as the rest of us were concerned, Andy would be walking to his stand in urine-soaked long johns.

Andy is a big, fit guy. He played high school hockey. The walk to his stand was a good mile, and he had to cross a swamp right before he reached his stand. Thus, he made the trek in his knee-high rubber boots while toting his pac boots, food, coffee, his rifle, a sleeping bag and God knows what other paraphernalia in a military duffel bag. Never in my life have I seen anyone carry so much gear to go deer hunting. He probably could have survived out there for days.

So there it was, opening morning. In Wisconsin, the holidays rank Christmas first, gun deer season second, and then everything else just kind of falls wherever. I have had nightmares about waking up on opening morning only to see that it's already light out and I've missed the magic of watching the sun rise on that most sacred of hunting holidays.

Well, then there's Andy. Like a good and proper person, Andy dressed in minimal layers for the long hike to his stand so he wouldn't get sweaty and cold while he sat. Once he reached his little stacked-log stand, he removed his rubber boots and exchanged them for some oversized pac boots like you might find on an expedition to the South Pole. He reached into that duffle bag to pull out his blaze-orange hunting parka, which he donned, and his sleeping bag, which he would slip into once he started to cool down from the long hike.

Finally, he likely sat in darkness, counting down the minutes to legal shooting time. Then, and only then, did he turn his attention to his 7mm rifle. Loading up early simply isn't legal. It was at that point that he made a tragic discovery. There was no bolt in his bolt-action rifle!

His wife didn't like the fact that there were guns in the house, especially considering they had small children. So Andy removed the bolt from his rifle so no one would get into trouble.

So now, here he sat; the sun just starting to glow on the eastern horizon, with his bolt tucked away in his gun case at Ryan and Jen's house a mile away.

Anyone else – anyone else – would have gone into full-on panic mode. Me? I'd have vaulted out of that stand and sprinted, huffing and puffing, the mile to the house. Maybe, just maybe, I could make it back before that opening morning dawn magic faded away. I'd have been ripe with sweat, out of breath and frantic. My blood pressure would be through the roof. NO ONE MESSES WITH MY OPENING DAY!!!

But not Andy. Oh, I'm sure he was disappointed. But he just sat. His first thought was not of himself and his inability to shoot a deer if it walked past him. Rather, he thought of Jen. He would have to pass her stand on the way back to the house to get his bolt and he didn't want to disturb her hunt. Seriously, who does that?

So he waited patiently in his stand for an hour or two with no means to do anything but sit and watch the chickadees until the early morning magic was over. Then he calmly walked back to the house and retrieved the bolt.

Now naturally, when he told the story that evening, we had to give him some good-natured ribbing. And that incident, combined with the early morning long john incident, earned him the nickname, "The Boltless Dribbler." It seems kind of a cruel thing to name him, especially considering his selfless sacrifice to sit without the means to shoot, just so he wouldn't ruin someone else's hunt.

Yeah, definitely a cruel name. But then, we're kind of jerks.

Amanda's Buck

Even before Amanda met me, she was into fishing, especially ice-fishing. She had all her own gear – rods, reels, tackle, electronics, a portable ice shack and even a better ice auger than I have. With our mutual love of fishing, it was never hard to come up with a date idea.

But as our first summer together wound down, little did Amanda know she was about to become a hunting widow. Amanda's family doesn't hunt much, although there is a legendary story about her father serving a porcupine for dinner without admitting what kind of meat it was until years later.

But I digress.

As I spent less time fishing and more time hunting that first fall, Amanda and I spent less time outdoors together. I didn't think much about it. I was just ensconced in my usual routine of chasing small game and then getting ready for gun-deer season. But Amanda must have been thinking about our lack of time together. Finally, one day she started asking questions about deer hunting. She'd never been hunting, and although she thought the ducks I killed were cute, she thought she could kill a deer.

Hint, hint.

Finally, she asked if I would take her deer hunting.

She may have gotten more than she bargained for. Minnesota has an apprentice hunter program, which allows rookie hunters to forego the otherwise mandatory hunter-education course. You must be accompanied by a mentor, however, and it becomes the mentor's job to ensure that the rules of hunter safety are taught and followed.

So instead of being just a spectator, Amanda quickly became a participant.

Amanda already owned a .243, which she had won at a Ducks Unlimited banquet. Outfitting her with hunting clothing was a real treat for her the moment she found out that blaze-pink camouflage is legal; like she really needed to buy more pink clothing. I bought and erected a two-person ladder stand. And after a trip to the rifle range, we soon learned Amanda was a natural marksman. Only a few weeks after the idea of trying deer hunting entered her mind, it was time for Amanda's first hunt.

Although Minnesota has a 16-day rifle season, with work obligations, busy schedules and juggling kids, we had just three days to hunt together. We wouldn't even hit the woods until the second weekend.

Finally, the day arrived. Winter had come early, and already a couple inches of snow blanketed the ground. Our morning sit, perched 15 feet into the frosty air, was anything but warm. But Amanda was a trooper and didn't complain. However, by noon, the only deer we'd seen was the one eating under my birdfeeder when we rolled down my driveway in the dark. It was time for a change in tactics.

With fresh snow on the ground, I decided we'd try to cut a track and see if we could track down a buck – no easy task, even for an experienced hunter. We'd be going straight from the minors to the big leagues in an attempt to kill a deer. Although we did cut a fresh track, we ran out of daylight before we caught up with the deer.

Day 2 was no more productive than the first day. It seemed there were more hunters in the woods than deer. After enduring another deer-less sit, spotting a hunter walking past our stand and hearing a close shot, we decided to try another spot in the afternoon. Unfortunately, we ran into yet another hunter in my old ace-in-the-hole spot. Amanda was quickly getting a lesson in the frustrations of public-land hunting.

Day 3 was a Monday and we hoped we'd have the woods to ourselves. The spot where I'd set up our ladder stand was looking like a dud, so we sat on the ground in another place where I've had success over the years.

We'd been sitting for less than an hour when suddenly, a deer materialized at the base of the hill below us. I quickly tugged Amanda's sleeve and pointed downhill, but as soon as I spotted the deer, it ducked into a thick copse of evergreens. Soon, a second deer appeared, then a third and a fourth. But as soon as they materialized, they disappeared in the balsam grove.

"Now what?" Amanda hissed.

"We wait," is all I could think to say.

I assumed that in a matter of seconds, the deer would push through the trees and continue moving from right to left.

"Rest your gun against this tree," I directed. "And get ready. They should pop out any second."

But the seconds turned to minutes. Occasionally we'd catch a glimpse of movement within the trees. Those deer – all four of them – were only 75 yards away. But we couldn't even make them out. What were they? Since there were four of them, I assumed they were does and fawns. But it was the heart of the rut, and where there are does, it doesn't take long for a buck to appear. I reasoned there probably wasn't a buck in the bunch…if there was, he'd be chasing them all over. Although Amanda's tag was good for any deer, she'd made up her mind that she wanted a buck. All we could do was hope that sooner or later, a buck would show up on their backtrail.

The deer were in no hurry to leave their little refuge, which probably wasn't more than 15 or 20 yards wide. Finally, one stepped into the open, but before Amanda could even find it in her scope, it slipped back into the cover from which it had come. The chess match continued, and it was the deer's move.

After 45 long minutes, I wasn't even sure if the deer were still there. We hadn't seen them for quite a while, although we hadn't seen them leave, either. Finally, they exited the backside of the cover without ever giving us a good look.

And that was the extent of Amanda's inaugural deer season. Four deer seen, barely. No bucks identified and no shots fired. At least she'd experienced the thrill of seeing deer sneak through the woods undetected and that heart-in-your-throat moment of excitement. But now it was back to work for her.

Two mornings later, I hunted the same spot without Amanda. I was perched in my climber, overlooking that little copse of balsams where the deer had played cat and mouse with us. Twenty minutes after legal shooting time a deer walked through the same patch of balsams, only this time, on a mission. As soon as it emerged, I saw antlers, even in the dim morning light.

The buck was on the move, heading right for me, and more importantly, heading right for the tracks I'd laid down not 40 minutes ago. In seconds, he'd cut those tracks and probably high-tail it out of there.

I had mere seconds to make a decision, but a million thoughts tore through my head.

My first thought was Amanda. Why did this buck have to be here now? Where was he two days ago? Do I shoot? Should I let him go? Amanda couldn't hunt anymore this year, but what about next year? Could he make it through and would we see him again?

The reality of the situation is we hunt public land. We don't have trail cameras out (for fear they'd be stolen). We don't know which bucks are around or how frequently they show up. Maybe the buck is a regular, but maybe he's just passing through. And if I let him go, would he be shot by another hunter? Maybe not. Hey, he'd made it through the first 11 days of the season.

Amanda endured cold, snowy conditions during her inaugural deer hunt. Her pink camouflage was a fashion statement as much as a safety precaution. And the eyepatch helped her look through her scope. Despite a few deer sightings, her tag went unfilled.

This 9-point buck appeared in the same grove of balsams where Amanda had seen four deer just two days earlier. Although I felt guilty about getting a chance at a buck when Amanda hadn't, the obvious choice was to embrace the opportunity.

Here he was. A buck in front of me. Just 60 yards away in the wide open. Amanda was done hunting for the year. I still had a tag. And what's more, those days I'd hunted with Amanda, I didn't even carry a gun. This was only my second day to hunt.

It was an easy decision; an obvious decision. I shot. The buck trotted off and I heard him crash just out of sight.

My first text went to Amanda. Oh, I gloated a little that I'd just shot a buck from her spot. But in reality, I felt sheepish. If that scenario unfolded a thousand times, I'd want Amanda to be there every time. No question about it. But I didn't get that choice. All I had was a decision to shoot or pass. I think I made the right call.

That 9-pointer will soon be on my wall; a stoic reminder of that hunt. But even though Amanda never even laid eyes on that deer until she saw him in the back of my truck, in my mind, he'll always be her buck.

Deer & Deer Hunting
February 2020

Opie's Antics

On more than one occasion, while sitting around a campfire or philosophizing over a beer, Aaron Opsteen and I have pondered, "How have we lived this long when we're this dumb?" Surely, by now, given the stupid things we do, we should have been long since weeded out of the gene pool.

It would seem the day God handed out common sense, "Opie" and I were probably giggling at some fart joke, showing each other funny Facebook memes or trying to come up with a burn so ruthless it would forever silence the other guy. You ever see *Dumb and Dumber*? Stick Jim Carrey and Jeff Daniels in the woods and that's us.

For all his idiocy, I actually have to give Opie some credit (although it pains me to do it). The guy is actually pretty handy to have around. He likes to prep and plan. He's the kind of guy who sets up camp as soon as we get to our campsite. Meanwhile, I'm so eager to get out fishing that I rush to launch the boat, figuring I can set up camp in the dark after the fish are done biting. Fast-forward a few hours and there's Opie, relaxing with a hot chocolate under his perfectly tarped tent, watching me stumble in the dark with a very dim headlamp – tent poles and tent tangled in a bird's nest. In the pouring rain.

Opie packs his truck a full week before a hunting trip (no exaggeration), checks and double-checks his entire gear list and will probably have an extra fork, pair of socks or deer rifle for a hapless sap like me who packed everything at the last possible moment and then forgot half of the things I should have brought. One time, while trying to sleep in the back of his truck topper, I was freezing my butt off because I'd forgotten to bring a sleeping pad. After I tossed and turned for an hour, he finally gave me an extra blanket he'd been using on top of his sleeping bag, although the gesture may have been disingenuous. I suspect he really gave me the blanket just so I'd stop complaining and he could get some sleep.

His resourcefulness is why, a few years ago when I wanted to do a backcountry shed hunt for moose antlers, he was the first guy I called. "It's like this," I explained. "We're gonna have to hike several miles and cross two rivers just to get to our starting point. I figure you'll have to drive about 8 hours to get here. We go in Friday morning, set up camp and we'll have just one day to shed hunt. Then we'll have to break camp super early Sunday morning, and then, God forbid if we're actually successful, we'll have to haul heavy packs all that way back, so you can be on the road for the long drive home. I figure you're just the right amount of dumb to do this with me."

It didn't take more than a nanosecond to convince him this was a good idea. And unfortunately, we did find a half-dozen moose antlers, which were a real pain to haul out.

So far, he seems like a pretty handy guy to have along, right? Maybe I'm giving him too much credit. Although he can be relied upon to gather truckloads of firewood for just a one-night camping trip, his eagerness to collect wood can, at times, cloud his judgment. He once made me paddle to shore on a canoe trip because he saw a dried, limbless log that would be perfect fuel for the campfire. It was too long to fit in the canoe, so I watched in slow-motion horror (fully realizing what was about to happen) as he raised the log over his head like a maul and slammed it down on a rock. The log broke, all right, and part of it bounced up and hit him under the chin, dropping him instantly to his knees. Medical help was hours away. Luckily the log didn't do any major damage. Might have actually knocked some sense into him.

A similar incident occurred with a post pounder. He was driving in a T-post in a creek bed. He raised the heavy, two-handled pounder high and somehow managed to bring it down on his head. He had the presence of mind to stagger out of the creek to shore, knowing his son wouldn't be able to remove him from the water if he passed out. Fear not, no brains seeped out of the gash in his head, because I'm not sure there were many to begin with. Only nine staples later and his head was as good as new!

Much of my time with Opie is spent deer hunting. In the woods, he's a real gem. One time he decided to move his ladder stand during a midday lull. He was only moving it a short distance, so he decided to transport it in one piece, rather than disassemble it, only to reassemble it a few yards away. He laid the stand down horizontal, then tried to find a good balance point as he picked up the stand and rested it on his shoulders. Opie is about as big around as a flagpole, and the ladder slid down over his shoulders, pinning his arms at his sides.

"I was panicking!" he told me that night after our hunt. "I didn't know what to do! My arms were stuck. Finally, I leaned the stand against a tree and was able to pry it off. I was worried I was gonna have to call you to remove it!"

*Opie, left, was "just the right amount of dumb" to accompany me on an excru-
ciating moose shed hunt. He drove 16 hours round-trip, hiked several miles and
crossed two rivers, just to get to the starting point on a one-day shed hunt.*

"If you had called me," I assured him, "I'd have dropped your pants
around your ankles, taken a picture and then after I uploaded it to Facebook, I'd have helped you remove the stand."

Opie is a fast hiker and sweats a lot. So one morning, he was walking
to his stand completely topless, carrying his jacket and long johns.
Before he climbed into his stand, he decided he needed to answer nature's
call. He was on a hill, so as he squatted down, he grabbed two saplings
for support. The first sapling immediately uprooted. At this point, he was
too committed to the activity at hand to move, so he clung to the second
sapling, which was now bearing his entire weight. Slowly, this tree also
began to uproot. Sweat beaded up on his bald head and his eyes grew wide
as he realized the levity of the situation. As the little tree gave way, Opie
desperately clutched at it, choking up frantically as its roots pulled free
of the frozen soil. Ultimately, Opie went ass over teakettle, completely
topless and pants around his ankles, down the snowy hill. How he avoided
landing in his own excrement, I'll never know.

Oh, and by the way, the sapling incident and the ladder stand debacle
happened the same day. It's a wonder the guy ever shoots a deer.

Opie insists on hunting in hilly areas and he likes to be in the brush.

Opie hunts on terrain that would make mountain goats blush. Here, I help him (above) move his buck up a steep hill.

Despite moments of bumbling through the woods, Opie has experienced success on remote, big-woods deer hunts. He rattled in this 9-pointer and another smaller buck at the same time. The small buck busted him, but the big one lagged behind. This buck was 9.5 years old!

Never mind that there's a clearing a couple hundred yards away where a guy could get an open shot at a buck and not have to literally ride it down a snowy hill and then try to pull it up Mount Everest on the other side of the ravine. One time after he shot a buck, the hill was so slick and so steep that we couldn't get enough traction to get the buck to the top. So we used our feeble brains and wrapped a rope around a tree at the top. One guy marched down the hill with the rope, using the tree like a pulley, while the other stood at the top of the hill to grab the deer. Me? I hunt on top of a hill and it's downhill the whole way back to the truck. Duh.

A couple years back, Opie decided to rattle during rifle season. He was still standing up, antlers still in hand, when a buck rushed in. It caught him completely off guard and there was nothing he could do. The deer had him pegged and it snorted and bounded off. Chaps my ass that a minute later a much larger buck responded to the calling as well. That buck was much harder to drag up the hill. I have the permanent back pain to prove it.

A few years back, I got a single trail camera photo of a giant buck. The following spring, I tried unsuccessfully to find the buck's sheds. A year later, Opie managed to find a shed off this monster. He told me where

Opie shot a forkhorn buck and it trotted off. Minutes later, he spotted a forkhorn, assumed it was the same deer and shot it. It turned out to be two nearly identical bucks. I had to burn a nonresident tag to get him out of a jam; a fact that I'll always hold over his head as leverage.

he found it, and the following day, I matched it up. I've now found three sheds off this buck, plus we'd have never even known about this deer, had it not been for *my* trail camera, but since Opie found the first shed, the unwritten rule of shed hunting says he gets the match. It was not easy to give up the second-biggest shed I've ever found. Jerk!

Opie is an early riser, while I'm a night owl and he loves to text me early in the morning when he knows I'm sleeping. He is also the only person who has ever flung a deer leg at me and hit me in the chest. So far.

Perhaps the worst thing he's done to me (up to this point) happened on the second day of rifle season a few years back. After sitting all day on opener without a deer sighting, a hot doe lured a forkhorn buck right to him. The buck was only 12 paces from his ground blind when he fired. The buck bolted and disappeared over the hill. Opie waited a few minutes to give the deer time to expire. A couple minutes later, he was surprised to see a small buck crest a hill to his left. He raised his rifle, saw that it was a forkhorn and realized he must have missed, but was getting a second chance. He fired and all was quiet. Minutes later, as he followed the tracks in the snow, he realized what had happened. It was two different bucks with identical racks.

Up until this point, Opie had been texting me the details of what was happening just over the hill. Now he called me.

"Um, I've got a little problem," he began. "You better unload your gun. I need your tag."

I ambled over the hill a short distance to his ground blind.

I spoke first as I approached him. "So you'll never guess what happened," I began. "As I was walking over here, by sheer dumb luck, I walked right up to the biggest buck I've ever seen. He must have thought I was a doe. I got within 30 yards of him and he just stood there and looked at me. Huge beams. Super wide. Points everywhere. I've never seen anything like him! He was truly a dream buck, but I knew you had two bucks down, so I passed on him. I'm happy to burn my expensive, nonresident tag on your second tiny little forkhorn. That's just the kind of guy I am."

"Shut up and give me your tag!" he replied.

Deer & Deer Hunting
October 2022

Hunting With Noah

I first met Noah when he was just a little shaver. I had recently taken a new job five hours from my hometown. The move was a big change. I had to learn my way around a new city. I had no clue about the local hunting and fishing hotspots. And I didn't know many people. Most intriguing to a small-water angler such as myself was the mystery of fishing on that big freshwater sea known as Lake Superior, which mesmerized me every time I gazed out at it in my newly adopted home. And right there is where Noah's dad, Jon, comes into the picture.

Jon was a new co-worker. I don't remember the first time we met, but when I inquired about fishing on the Big Pond, I was directed to him. Jon had spent a few years working as a first mate on charter boats and had hung out with a lot of the old-time captains. He knew how to fish Superior.

I machine gun-fired questions at Jon about Lake Superior fishing. I just had to know everything I could learn about fishing out there: the lures, the techniques, the gear and of course, big-water boating. After weeks of pestering Jon, I told him I was ready to fish Superior. My muskie rod would serve as a Dipsy Diver rod and my giant muskie net would just barely haul in those massive Lake Superior fish I'd catch (the first of which was a 15-inch salmon). I didn't own downriggers yet, but with cold water temperatures, Jon assured me just running stickbaits near the surface would be OK. My final question for him dealt with the marine forecast. The waves were projected to be up to 3 feet. Jon's final words, when probed if the lake was fishable in my little 16-foot boat: "You *will* get wet." That we did. But a friend and I landed a coho and a lake trout and we were thrilled.

Jon quickly became like an adopted father to me, teaching me about Lake Superior fishing, helping me with projects and even letting me live with him for a few months. That fall, I was invited to his deer camp. This leased camp was a hunter's paradise. It had a network of trails to walk for grouse, a beaver pond that always held a few wood ducks, and of course, a couple hundred acres of prime deer hunting land. That's what my eyes saw, but Jon looked at things differently. To him, deer camp was a place to be a guy. He could escape work responsibilities, get out of the house and drink a few beers. What's more, it was the perfect venue for outdoor cooking.

Jon's famous line is, "My trophies are on the grill." He always had some kind of meat sizzling on the grill, a roast chugging away in a smoker or a smorgasbord of meat and vegetables simmering for his famous garbage can feasts. To me, deer hunting had always been about shooting deer. Give me two granola bars and I'll sit all day until I shoot a deer or darkness falls. Jon's style, I learned, was to hunt for a couple hours in the morning, then get something cooking back at camp, watch football and let the other guys shoot the deer.

During Noah's first deer season, I lucked out and shot a buck opening morning, so I headed out to Jon's deer camp the next day. Noah's eyes lit up when I arrived. "Dad, can I hunt with Joe this evening?" he asked.

I was flattered, but I pulled Jon aside and explained I didn't want to take away that father-son moment of Noah's first deer if we got lucky.

"Get the kid a deer," Jon replied.

That afternoon, sitting in a box blind on stilts, Noah was getting bored. We hadn't seen anything. And there was no smartphone to keep him entertained. Eventually he leaned his head against the wall out of sheer boredom. So when a deer showed up a while later, I had to tug at his hood to alert him. Luckily, we didn't spook the deer and Noah shot it.

After that, Noah and I bonded. I took him canoeing the following summer. We went muskie fishing. We even fished and camped with Jon and his crew a couple times.

But Noah was growing up. Soon, he graduated from high school and went off to college. For a few years, I rarely saw him.

In the meantime, Jon's interest in the outdoors was waning. He hardly fished. He sold his boat. And eventually, as Noah and his cousins grew up and moved away, the deer camp was dismantled. That part was heartbreaking. Those guys had truly created something special. Four different boys shot their first deer at "the land," but more than that, it was the camaraderie of sleeping in musty old campers, watching football on a generator-operated TV and most of all, walking inside the shack to a wall of steam from Jon's cooking after a cold day of hunting.

The first year after the camp was dismantled was a sad one. The guys had a really good thing going there. So imagine my surprise when Noah texted me that fall.

In my mind, I didn't see Noah as becoming an outdoorsman. He hadn't had much success hunting, and now the camp was gone so there was less incentive to hunt. Jon no longer fished at all. And while at college, Noah

Noah likes to hunt in comfort. His flip-over ice fishing shack doubles as a ground blind during deer season.

had other priorities. But after graduation, he circled back to it. To me, this was a kid who needed a mentor. We had trouble aligning our schedules, but we made it out duck hunting once. When Noah informed me he'd be deer hunting back at the land, even though the camp was gone, it warmed my heart.

I hunted elsewhere for the first few days of season, but hunting was slow, so I asked if I could join Noah for a couple days. He hadn't killed anything, but he'd seen a doe that "winded him."

When I arrived to hunt with him, I was amazed at what I saw. Noah's

SUV had become a garage on wheels. It was absolutely overflowing with hunting and fishing paraphernalia! With an early freeze, he had to make sure he had all his ice fishing stuff, in addition to his deer hunting equipment. In fact, his truck may be the only one I've ever seen that's messier than mine and I wouldn't doubt that if you dug through the layers of sporting goods you'd find open-water walleye lures, paddles, an anchor, dried-up minnows and maybe even a mummified perch!

You had to admire his setup. He was deer hunting from his flip-over ice shack. He removed the windows and sat on a padded, sliding seat with the heater running in complete comfort.

However, when I realized he had set up in the middle of an open field – and only 5 yards from his truck – I had to question whether that doe had truly winded him or if she was just startled by what she saw when she stepped out of the pines only 50 yards away.

After sitting in a tree stand one frigid morning and then making an unsuccessful deer drive to Noah, I sat with Noah in his ice shack/deer stand at midday. You could see the apple hadn't fallen far from the tree. Whereas my deer hunting is focused on killing a deer, Noah's is all about comfort. Inside the shack was a double sunflower heater that kicked out enough BTUs to heat a two-story house. He had a few cans of pop that had frozen in his truck overnight, but that was no problem. He hung his ice scoop from one of the cross members of the shack, directly over the heater. The can nestled perfectly in the scoop and in no time his Popsicle became a beverage. He had an entire tub of trail mix to last him, but for the main course, he'd brought leftover tater tot hot dish, wrapped in foil, which he warmed over the heater. I was impressed. Noah really had it all figured out. This was much better than sitting in a tree stand, although I did suggest that maybe he should at least move his truck out of the field, which he did.

For a couple hours we sat and talked, all cozy in the steamy shack. We caught up on each other's lives and vowed to do some serious ice-fishing, which I was pleased to learn Noah had really gotten into. It was midday, so I assumed our chances of seeing a deer were low, especially considering we had just pushed an adjacent strip of woods. We jabbered, looked at old photos on our phones and just had a good time. But one thing had been nagging at me for a while: the removable windows in the shack were closed and steamed up. There was no way we would be able to remove the Velcro windows without spooking a deer. I decided we should at least make an effort to hunt, even if seeing a deer seemed unlikely.

So we opened the steamed-up windows, letting in a draft of arctic air. I told Noah he should have his rifle a little more accessible, too. After all, you might only have a few fleeting moments to get a shot. Noah agreed. He turned around to grab his cased rifle inside the fishing sled. After moving our jackets around, he finally realized something: we had been "hunting" in the shack now for two hours, but neither one of us had a gun! Our rifles were both tucked safely in their cases in Noah's truck, now 75 yards away. When we discovered our folly, we laughed until we had tears in our eyes. There's something to be said for hunting in comfort, but at some point you need to at least *try* to shoot a deer!

The important thing is, after a brief hiatus and against the odds, Noah has caught the outdoors bug, and he wants to find success in the woods and waters. We'll just have to work on those hunting skills a bit.

Outdoor News
March 13, 2020

A Hunter is Born

If I live to be 50, I'll never understand women. I suppose, in this day of advanced medicine and increasing life expectancy, 50 years seems like a pretty meager goal. But that modest age is irreversibly entwined with my inability to understand the other gender.

It took longer than it should have for me to realize that when a female asks if something makes her look fat, the answer is an emphatic "no!" I think the proper way to answer that question would be to give her a split-second glance and say something like, "That outfit makes you look like the prettiest belle at the ball."

You don't even need to look at her to know the answer is "no." That response should come automatically. But women are so sensitive, you can answer this trick question incorrectly, even when you think you've given the proper response. You have to at least glance at her so she knows you're not just saying she doesn't look fat, but if you look at her for even a millisecond too long, she'll think you had considered that maybe she does, indeed, look a bit chubby.

Oh, and another thing: there is a language barrier across the genders. "Fine" in man speak is not a parallel translation in the female dialect. In fact, those words are complete antonyms. Use the wrong translation and you'll be punched in the shoulder or kicked in the shin. Even if your gal is petite, those beatings pack a wallop. Thus, the reason I feel I'll be doing well to make it to 50.

I don't know why Amanda decided she wanted to go deer hunting. Hunting was not a big part of her family. Her dad and brother formerly hunted, but they held only a passing interest in the sport and it had been years since either pursued deer. I suppose dating me was the impetus for her desire to hunt. She already had a natural love of fishing, even before she met me. She had all her own ice fishing gear, some of which was better than my own equipment. But hunting would be a new realm for her.

Men and women are wired differently when it comes to the outdoor sports, in my experience. When guys go fishing, the ultimate goal is to catch fish. Oh sure, they like hanging out and perhaps tipping back a few beers on the water, but at the end of the day, if they haven't caught some fish, the outing wasn't successful.

Women, on the other hand, enjoy the camaraderie and the experience. They cheer on each other and try to share their knowledge to help make everyone a better angler. They don't want anything "mansplained" to them — guys hovering around and constantly giving advice. But for them, it's OK when a woman imparts knowledge to another woman. Success is measured by the amount of fun had by all, and if any fish make it into the boat, even small ones, everyone shares in the success.

Now, that scenario isn't 100 percent accurate, but it seems to hold true in a lot of situations. Women just enjoy the outdoors for different reasons than men. And I'll give them credit, women are very patient and detail-oriented, which serves them well while hunting or fishing. They're also not too macho to ask for help and they take constructive criticism better than men; especially if it comes from another woman. For these and myriad other reasons, women often excel in outdoor sports.

So, for reasons known only to her, Amanda asked if I would take her deer hunting. The joke may have been on her, however, because Minnesota has a hunting mentorship program, through which individuals can hunt without taking the normally required hunter safety course, as long as their mentor stays within arm's length. Amanda wasn't just going hunting; she was about to be a hunter! And of course, the second she found out that she could wear blaze pink clothing instead of the traditional blaze orange, she immediately went on a pink shopping spree!

Our first season was a struggle. Amanda didn't have much time to hunt and deer sightings were few. Plus, she had a hard time looking through her scope with just one eye, so she carried along an eye patch for her non-scope eye, which made peering through the scope easier. That move earned her the nickname, "The Pink Pirate." We did manage to see a few does, but Amanda's tag went unfilled that first year.

The following season, things looked much better. For one thing, we wouldn't be hunting in the woods, where visibility is limited and deer are close and easily spooked when you do see them. We had gotten permission to hunt over a farm field where deer appear each night to feed. Tom, the landowner, laughed when I showed up before season to do some scouting.

"All you have to do is watch the field," he explained. "There will be deer there every night."

As I soon learned, I was trying to overcomplicate a sure bet.

On our first evening, Amanda and I watched the field, waiting for deer to appear. Perhaps an hour before dark, a doe and fawn emerged from behind a row of pines and began grazing on alfalfa. They fed trustingly, never realizing they were being watched by predators.

Amanda watched intently, enjoying the encounter. Although her tag was good for any deer, she wanted to hold out for a buck. We had three evenings to hunt, and if she had to settle for a doe, she wouldn't do it until the final evening.

As it turned out, her chance at a buck came quicker than expected.

The doe and fawn were still feeding in the field when Mr. Big arrived. Well, OK, he wasn't exactly big. In human terms, he was a teenager. He had just grown his first set of antlers that summer. They consisted of 5-inch spikes on either side of his head. His was a pretty meager rack. But he was a buck.

Amanda, who had been so calm while watching the doe and fawn, suddenly began to breathe heavily when she spotted the young buck. She trembled as she raised the rifle. She struggled to see the buck in her rifle scope. A couple weeks earlier, at the shooting range, everyone who watched her shoot was impressed. She was a natural marksman and once we had her scope on target, she regularly hit the bull's-eye. However, right now she couldn't even see through the scope, and if she could have, she was so unsteady she would have struggled to hit the broad side of a barn.

Even though she was leaning on a solid rest, the rifle barrel wobbled from side to side. At the shooting range, she was calm and steady and she shot with military precision. But this was the real world. She didn't know it, but something deep within her psyche, going all the way back to her caveman ancestors, was emerging. That "fight or flight" response was welling up inside her as she prepared to kill her prey and it was rattling her visibly. All she had to do was settle the crosshairs on the buck and pull the trigger. I know she was capable of making that shot. I'd watched her do it repeatedly at the shooting range. But things are different with a live target. After probably a minute or more of struggling to find the deer in the scope, she finally pulled the trigger. The young buck bounded off unscathed.

A flood of emotions washed over her. She was disappointing that she had missed the deer. And she commented repeatedly on how difficult it was to make that shot in the heat of the moment. It wasn't like being at the shooting range. It was real and nerve-racking and different. She hadn't killed her deer, but the experience had taken hold of her. She had gotten a taste of that moment when you come in contact with your prey and the encounter was exciting and new. Now she was more determined than ever to shoot a buck!

The following night we were back, but no buck appeared. Originally, Amanda had said she would shoot any deer on her last evening. However, after her encounter with the young buck, she wasn't going to settle for a doe on the third evening. It was a buck or nothing. Once again, no buck appeared on the third night, although we did see some does. I thought that, just like last year, her season would end in defeat. Little did I know we were just getting started.

The memory of that buck gnawed at Amanda. Originally, on the following evening, we were supposed to help Amanda's brother, Josh, move into his new house. In fact, Amanda had reminded me not to forget just the day before. But on the fourth day, she sent me a text: "Let's hunt at Tom's tonight!"

"What about your brother?" I responded.

"He can move himself!"

So Josh was on his own.

The fourth night turned into a fifth. And a sixth. The sixth night was a pivotal one. Once again, does appeared in the field. We had watched them for more than an hour. It was growing dark and it was getting hard to see, although the legally mandated quitting time for the day was still a few minutes away. Amanda unloaded her rifle and tucked it into its case. Just as she did so, another deer entered the field, followed by another. Even in the waning light, I could clearly see both were bucks! The first buck was a nice one, sporting a decent rack. But the second one, oh the second one, was the buck of dreams. The barrel-chested bruiser strode into the field with confidence. He knew he was the boss of the woods. His antlers spread beyond his ears, with thick tines jutted up from heavy main beams.

In about two seconds flat, Amanda's rifle was back out of the case. She reloaded and peered through the scope. I put my fingers in my ears, expecting at any moment to hear the rifle roar. I waited. And waited. But the expected rifle blast didn't come. The sky grew darker. The bucks became mere silhouettes. At long last, Amanda lowered the rifle.

"I just can't see him through the scope!" she hissed.

I was dejected on the inside, but I dared not show it. Oh, how I wished her first buck had been a giant! The light was dim and making the shot wouldn't have been easy. Still, I know that I could've found a way. But this wasn't about me. It was about Amanda, and she was disappointed, too. She knew that buck was a monster.

But one of the most important parts of hunting is gun safety. If you can't see your target well or make a good shot, you're better off not shooting. It would've been a horrible thing to have wounded the deer and not recovered it. As badly as she wanted to shoot it, she made the right call.

After that there was no turning back. Amanda's three-day hunt miraculously stretched into yet another day. She wanted a buck bad! This time, however, this really was her last day. Tom had friends coming to hunt. In fact, he had foregone his own hunting so that Amanda could hunt. We had one final chance.

On our last sit, many thoughts went through our minds. We thought about that spike buck from the first day. We talked about the thrill of watching the does and fawns feed every night. And of course, the vision of that monster buck – the one that got away – was always at the forefront of our minds. But as the clock ticked down, it looked like we were out of chances. Two does and a fawn fed in the alfalfa – where was their male suitor?

It had been a fun season. Amanda had learned a lot. She'd discovered that trying to shoot at a live target isn't the same as shooting at the range. We'd come so close. We'd seen bucks and even got a shot at one. It really had been a pretty good season. But somehow it just wasn't enough to go home without a buck. We sat quietly, sullenly, dwelling on the impending reality of another deer-less season.

We had just a half-hour left to hunt when yet another buck entered the field. Amanda had sat with her head hung on that final sit, but this new buck sighting jolted her back to life. She had one more shot at redemption!

There was a purpose in her movements as she brought her rifle to her shoulder this time. That girl who fidgeted awkwardly with a rifle just days earlier was gone. Now she aimed confidently and deliberately. This time her nerves were under control and the rifle barrel held steady. At the rifle's report, the buck dropped in its tracks.

"You got him!" I exclaimed.

Amanda couldn't believe her eyes, but a brown blob lay still in the middle of the alfalfa field. Amanda unloaded the rifle and set it down. I gave her a bear hug and kissed her. We couldn't cover the distance across the field fast enough to get to her first buck. As she walked up on the deer, conflicting emotions bubbled out of her. For one thing, there was a bit of shock that she had gotten a third chance and this time had made good. There was probably relief, too. Night after night we'd been trying for a buck, and now she finally had one. As we knelt next to the fallen deer,

After a week of evening hunts, Amanda finally connected with her first buck on her final opportunity.

Amanda brushed the deer's gray winter coat. There is always that moment of remorse when you realize that you've snuffed out the candle of life and Amanda was sad for the deer. But more than anything, she was elated. She had become part of the fraternity of hunters. No longer was she a spectator; she was an active participant. Amanda gushed about the experience. The buck wasn't the monster we'd seen a couple days earlier, but Amanda couldn't have been prouder.

I don't know why Amanda chose to deer hunt. I guess I could ask her. But as I stood there watching a girl kneel next to her first buck, the sheer joy and elation on her face was all the reason I needed.

Northern Wilds
November 2021

The Braggart

Give him some credit. The Braggart had sacrificed a lot. For years, he had hunted cushy farmland during the gun season. This was prime deer country, with deer sightings in the dozens each day. Probably the best deer hunting you could ask for outside of a ranch managed for trophy bucks and hunters with fat wallets.

But the Braggart wanted something different. He wanted to hunt where just seeing a deer is an accomplishment, and where camaraderie is more important than a sagging meat pole. He wanted to know the sweat that poured out of an overheated body on a long trudge through a swamp and the heft of a deer on a mile-long drag. Real deer hunting. His heart was in the right place and he joined his friends for a deer hunt "up north" on public land.

The party had been hunting the area for a few years. The group hunts hard, sitting all day long most days, and making drives when they can sit no longer. They earn any deer they kill, and there's no hesitation in shooting any deer – even a fawn. And just seeing a buck – any buck – would make a hunter the talk of camp.

The Braggart had it easy. The scouting was already done and the stand sites were chosen. He just had to show up.

Saturday, for the first time in his life, the Braggart didn't see a deer on opening day. It was a new experience; a humbling one. But he didn't mind helping his friends haul out their three deer, even if it was agonizing dragging them through a spongy swamp with water up to his knees and sometimes beyond. It seemed good and right, and for the first time he felt a share in the accomplishment, even if it wasn't his own.

The second day the Swamp Stand was open. The Rookie had sat there until 1 p.m. the first day without seeing a deer. It was ironic, too, because this was the area with the most deer sign, and everyone predicted it would be the hot stand. The Rookie killed his first deer – a doe – from a different stand Saturday evening, so the Braggart occupied the Swamp Stand the second morning.

At 8:30 a.m. on Day 2, a shot rang out from the Swamp Stand, with another shot coming two minutes later.

The Braggart killed this 8-pointer from the Swamp Stand on the second morning of deer season. He assumed the big-buck pot was as good as his.

"I'm gonna need help," the Braggart said over the radio.

"What did you shoot?"

"A doe," he replied.

The Braggart had just finished field dressing the doe when his partners showed up.

"Would you mind grabbing my orange hat?" he asked, gesturing toward a tree 30 yards away.

His companions were puzzled, but obliged. Suddenly, things became clear. Under the hat lay an 8-point buck!

"Well, you heard two shots, didn't ya?" the Braggart said smugly.

Everyone was stunned.

A small 6-pointer killed the previous season was the only buck the group had tagged in the preceding three years. Just the presence of a respectable deer in the area seemed almost unbelievable.

"Well, I might as well collect that big buck pool right now," the Braggart said, grinning. "Tell ya what, maybe while you're out hunting this afternoon, I'll go to the casino and blow it all!"

He was joking, of course, but there was truth to his ribbing. The 8-pointer

On my first deer hunt "up north," I was fortunate to kill a doe and an 8-pointer on the second morning. I may have bragged a little too soon.

seemed insurmountable.

The jabs continued on the way out of the woods – an audacious move, considering that at any point, his companions could have taught him a lesson by leaving him to haul out his two deer by himself over the 1.4-mile drag.

Back at camp, the Rookie announced he was pulling out that evening and he needed help quartering his deer so he could transport it in his car.

"I'll stay and help," the Braggart offered. "Besides, I've already filled my tags and I'd hate to have to start filling everyone else's!"

Everyone knew the Braggart was joking, but his "humor" was getting a little old. Even the Braggart began to sense he was taking things too far. And he had plenty of time to think about it after the Rookie left as he sat in camp alone.

Soon, it was dark. An hour later, still no one had returned to camp. Someone must have shot a deer.

Minutes later, the Sheriff rolled in, screeching to a halt in a cloud of dust.

"Get in!" he yelled.

He throttled the truck like a madman, finally coming to a sudden halt where the hunting party enters the woods. He began hiking in earnest and the Braggart struggled to keep pace. Not a word was spoken.

Andy shot this 11-point buck from the Swamp Stand the same day that I killed a doe and an 8-pointer from it. Not only was it his first buck; it earned him the camp's big-buck pool.

After 10 minutes of brisk walking, a light shone through the trees ahead and the Sheriff quickened his pace even more. Soon, the Braggart saw two figures struggling through the woods, clearly dragging a deer. As he drew closer, the Braggart saw huge smiles break through grimacing faces as the draggers strained at the rope.

"Hope you didn't blow that big buck pool at the casino this afternoon," Andy piped up, "Because that would be *my* big buck pool," he said with a huge smile as he showed off his first buck – an 11-pointer – killed from the same stand where the Braggart had killed the doe and 8-pointer earlier that morning.

The Braggart had been beaten and he knew it. And he said so as he congratulated the excited hunter, relieved him of his rope and began tugging his way back to camp.

Deer Hunters Equipment Guide 2006

Vic and Eunie

I showed up late to my cousin's wedding reception and ended up sitting down next to one of those relatives whom you only see once in a while at family gatherings: my great uncle Vic. I sat down moments before the main course was served.

Midway through my chicken breast, I paused long enough to ask Vic if he'd done any fishing lately before taking my next bite. I should have known better.

You don't ask a weathered old man a question and expect a simple answer. He finished chewing and leaned back in his chair. He proceeded to tell me, in drawn-out fashion, how he'd started his boat motor and an alarm bell went off. Two minutes later, still amidst the broken motor story, I finally put my fork down, realizing I wouldn't be taking my next bite any time soon. His green eyes were locked on me and I was afraid to eat under the capture of those eyes.

"I don't get out fishing too much anymore," he said without segue after the motor story. "But we sure used to have a lot of fun," he said in a musing, reminiscent voice that told me my chicken was going to get cold.

"You guys don't have fun like we used to – no, we used to have a lot of fun. We'd get to work and get the girls together, go over to someone's house, throw the rug in the corner and put on a record. We'd dance all night, and we didn't need beer or anything. 'Course, beer wasn't legal back then, but we had a lot of fun," he said, his glowing eyes dancing like the youths in his story and it was apparent that it was only physically that he was in the 21st Century.

At the end of the story, there was a long-enough lull for me to finish my meal. When Vic finished, he leaned back again, and happy to have an audience, resumed his stories.

He spoke of goose hunting on Lake Butte des Morts and pike fishing, (which I remembered is walleye fishing to my generation) behind his house on Lake Winnebago. But most of his stories centered on deer hunting.

Vic related his tales of making the trip to northern Wisconsin with his wife, Eunice, every year for deer season. He told me of 12-point bucks, an elk sighting and deer-less seasons endured through frigid temperatures.

But most of it centered on Eunie.

"I'm gonna be 82 come this October," he said. "I got bad knees, ya know." (He'd had surgery on both knees). "I wouldn't need to go anymore; I just go because she likes to go. She'll sit out there all day and never gets cold. She has a lot of fun."

"I've done pretty good," he continued. "I got a 12-point, a 10-point, an 8-point, a 6-point and a 4-point. I guess it'll probably never happen, but I always wanted to get a 14-point," he breathed through thick lips.

"I don't know," he said, his voice growing somber and serious. "My knees aren't as good as they used to be. I don't even get out fishing much anymore. Well ... maybe this will be my last year deer hunting ..."

A knot formed in my stomach. He didn't look at me after that. His eyes stared blankly at the tablecloth. It was as if he didn't understand the magnitude of his thoughts until he said them aloud.

Just then, my brother joined us and changed the subject. Maybe it was a good thing. Maybe it was better not to dwell on the conversation.

I didn't stay long after the DJ arrived, but I'm sure Vic and Eunie polkaed that night. I've seen them dance like two lovestruck newlyweds before.

I know that maybe it's just a pipe dream. Vic only saw one deer last year, but I wish that by some miracle this year, a 14-point buck would work its way through a blanket of fresh November snow, guided by some unknown force to a northern Wisconsin forest in which an 82-year-old man and his wife sit. Maybe Eunie would shoot the deer before Vic sees it. I know that Vic would be just as proud.

Maybe I'm dreaming, but miracles happen. I just hope that I can enjoy as many hunting seasons and have as much fun as Vic and Eunie.

Deer & Deer Hunting
Early 2000s

The Great, Not So Great, Deer Drive

It was getting late in the Wisconsin gun deer season and the meat pole was about as barren as a deer stand during the Packer game. For days now, Ryan, his wife Jen and their friend Andy had been hunting in northwestern Wisconsin to no avail. The deer weren't moving and there weren't many opportunities for a shot.

The pit of Ryan's stomach was as empty as his freezer. Whether it's deer, duck, grouse, fish or even mushrooms, Ryan prides himself on feeding his family from the fat of the land. With a plethora of both buck and doe tags, it was time to make something happen.

Ryan had devised a surefire scheme that would surely push a deer to Jen and Andy. He dropped to a knee like a quarterback, drawing up the deadly plan with a finger in the snow. Ryan's own deer stand would serve as the ambush point. This monstrosity of stacked logs would make a log cabin jealous. It's a veritable fortress against the wind and it is with some trepidation that I walk near it, wondering when and if a sleepy bear will ever decide it's the perfect place to spend the winter.

While in the stand, you have a lake to your back, which pretty much eliminates the need to turn around to look behind you. To the left is a boggy black spruce and tamarack swamp that rims the lake. Just a hundred yards or so to the left of the stand, a nearly imperceptible change in elevation alters the entire forest community and the swamp trees give way to an oak forest, which spreads out in front of the stand. To the right, a thick copse of alder and willow hug the lake and provide thick cover. This brushy area was the key to the drive.

After days of hunting pressure, Ryan reasoned, the deer would be tired of running from hunters, who could see and shoot at them from the relative openness of the oak forest. Those deer would be holed up in thick cover and that brush was just the ticket!

With some final parting advice, Ryan left Jen and Andy at his stand, circled wide out into the oaks, then looped around to the lakeside brush, which he would walk toward the stand in hopes of pushing deer to Jen and Andy.

The standers sat quietly with great anticipation. After days of fruitless sits, there's excitement in knowing that someone is actively pushing deer toward you and that at any moment, a deer could step into view!

Ryan crashed into the nearly impenetrable wall of brush. It would be impossible to slip through the tangled mess undetected, and that was just fine because he hoped to roust any deer holed up in there and send them toward his waiting standers.

Ryan picked his way through the dense stand. At times he had to get down on his knees to duck under horizontal branches. Sometimes all he could do was bulldoze his way through. It was a great sacrifice, but it would all be worth it if his plan worked like he hoped.

Just a few minutes into the brush, Ryan was thrilled to hear a shot, then another, from the direction of his stand. In those days, Jen shot a very short, modified, single-shot .44 rifle that made a distinct "pop," which was followed nearly immediately by Andy's louder .308. Ryan beamed as he continued on. Seconds later, a third shot roared from the stand. Then all was quiet.

Ryan paid his due diligence by completing the drive, but his legs could hardly carry him fast enough. He was just dying to hear what had happened.

Ryan finally emerged from the labyrinth of brush and hustled to his stand. Jen and Andy were out of the stand when he arrived, standing over their deer.

Five does and fawns had appeared, straight in front of the stand. They were moving along slowly, not too concerned. Andy whispered that Jen should shoot first. While she aimed, Andy steadied his rifle on the log stand as well, and as soon as she shot, Andy fired too. Two does dropped.

The remaining three deer bounded off a few steps, then stopped, unsure of what had just happened. One of them stopped in the open, and with two doe tags in his pocket, Andy dropped another deer.

Ryan was feeling pretty proud of himself. It had all worked out like clockwork. Except it didn't. All the deer had come from the tamarack and spruce swamp – on their own – from the other side of the stand. Nothing came out of the brush where Ryan was walking!

Outdoor News
Oct. 15, 2021

The Ramrod Traditionalist

I decided I wanted to get into muzzleloading, not because I had suddenly grown an interest in perfecting charges and patterning loads, but rather, just as a way to extend my deer season.

Truthfully, I didn't want to deal with the complexities of muzzleloading. I just wanted a simple setup that would help me enjoy more days afield, so I planned to buy an in-line muzzleloader. They're easy to clean and you don't have to mess around with measuring powder and all that crap. Plus, they shoot farther. A coworker, Jim, got wind of my desire for a muzzleloader and told me he had just the thing for me.

One day he invited me over to his house to have a look at this mechanical wonder. I was expecting a nice, high-quality used in-line. What he had looked like something he stole from Davy Crockett.

"This'll be perfect," Jim said of the .50-caliber Hawken caplock with the octagonal barrel. I wasn't so sure. This was not what I had in mind.

"Don't you have a good gun lying around, like one of those break-action in-lines?" I asked.

Jim raised an eyebrow and stared at me coldly. I had executed the cardinal sin of muzzleloading: I'd insulted a traditionalist.

"Good gun?" Jim retorted. "This here, my dear boy, is a *great* gun! It's the best gun you could own, outside of a flintlock," he assured me. "This thing'll drop a deer as well as any of that new-fangled crap, and carrying it around will make a man outta ya. You don't want any of that in-line city-boy crap."

Yikes. I'd crossed a definite line. I don't know if it was Jim's ensuing sales pitch or the fact that I thought I'd better not strain things at work, but I gave in and bought it.

The mound of odds and ends that came with it essentially doubled the amount of outdoor gear I own. There was so much stuff that as soon as I got home, reality set in. Sure, I wanted to shoot it, but I realized if I did, I'd probably blow my head off. It was time to put my machismo aside and ask for a hearty portion of help.

Luckily, Jim offered to teach me the ropes of muzzleloading, although probably for no other reason than to take an extra-long lunch break. But Jim is one of those guys who takes everything to the extreme. A simple pheasant gun won't suffice. He owns 23 shotguns, from 10 gauge to .410. Heck, ask to borrow a stupid paper clip from him and he'll offer you three different styles. So it goes without saying, when it comes to muzzleloading gear, he's got it all, but no modern stuff. Jim's a traditionalist, right down to the buckskin loincloth, which thankfully, I've never had the, er, pleasure of seeing.

One day at lunch, the mountain man and I dragged the old front-stuffer – plus an entire shopping bag of roundballs, percussion caps, nipple wrenches, ramrods and a million other things – down to the shooting range. The mountain of gear was daunting. I cowered behind the shooting bench like a boy who was nervous to shoot a rifle for the first time while Jim spread equipment across the table.

"It's really pretty simple," Jim told me as he sorted through the endless assortment of gear.

I was skeptical. How was this easier than stuffing a couple Pyrodex pellets down the barrel, followed by a jacketed bullet and then priming the gun with a 209 primer? There would be no powder to spill, no caps to drop and much less fussing around. With all these "traditional" items lying around, things were bound to get misplaced or mixed up. I wished there were a hospital closer to the shooting range.

"Let me show you," Jim said.

After recommending a powder charge and teaching me the all-important "powder, patch, ball" order, the gun was loaded and ready to fire. Jim slid his glasses up his nose, donned earmuffs and drew a bead on a target 25 yards downrange. The muzzleloader roared and in a moment, our world was a cloud of smelly white smoke.

Hmm. That really didn't seem so bad. In fact, I had to admit, this looked like fun, now that I actually had a sense of what was going on. I decided to give it a whirl. I reloaded under Jim's hawklike supervision and fired. This was much different than what I was used to, but it was actually kind of cool, if you didn't mind the smell of rotten eggs.

"Oh, and another thing," Jim continued. "You're gonna want to swab the barrel after a few shots, and you definitely need to give the gun a good cleaning when you get home tonight."

"No problem," I thought. Jim instructed me to take a patch, dob some solvent on it, then run it down the barrel with a patch jag. I couldn't believe the amount of fouling left in the bore! In fact, the ramrod fit pretty tightly after just a couple shots, but I swabbed the barrel and we were shooting again.

We fired a few more balls, but soon it was time to head back to work. Remembering Jim's advice to clean the gun as soon as I got home, I decided to swab out the barrel again to get some of that crap outta there before the barrel started to rust. We'd shot three or four times since cleaning the barrel, and now that ramrod fit tighter than a quarter in a nickel slot machine! I managed to jam the rod in, but getting it out was another matter.

"Aw, man, that thing is *in* there!" I exclaimed. "I can't get it out!"

This wasn't supposed to happen, Jim assured me. It made sense that what goes in must come out, but the wooden ramrod was definitely stuck. I tried pulling slowly and steadily. I tried jerking quickly. I twisted the rod. Finally, it came out … minus the cleaning jag!

"You idiot! You just unscrewed it!" Jim blurted.

Now we had a real dilemma. Using our heads, we were able to simply screw the ramrod back onto the jag, but the jag still wouldn't budge.

"Let me see that," Jim snapped as he snatched the gun from me.

Jim gave that gun everything he had. He pulled. He twisted. He tried jumping up and down and swearing. Nothing worked.

Then an evil smile spread slowly across Jim's face.

"Here," he said, extending the gun toward me. "You hang onto the gun, and I'll pull on the ramrod."

I really wanted that jag out of the barrel, but this was crazy! If it didn't seem so dangerous, I bet it would've been really funny, but Jim assured me there was no powder or bullet in the gun – which we had just fired prior to swabbing – and we seemingly had no other choice. With Jim gripping the ramrod and my hands clenching the gun, we squared off like two sumo wrestlers, circling around, tugging, doing anything we could think of to break the ramrod loose, but all to no avail. Disgusted, we put the gun back in the case, ramrod still in the barrel, and went back to work.

"Come over to my place after work and we'll get that thing outta there," Jim assured me.

A few hours later, I was at Jim's house, sheepishly holding the muzzleloader.

"I've got this CO_2 gizmo some techie gave me years ago," Jim said. "You screw it onto the nipple and it's supposed to blow your bullet out of the gun. I never used the stupid thing. Why would I? You'd have to be a moron to get a ball stuck down a barrel. 'Powder, patch, ball,' " he continued. "What's so hard about that? Well, maybe the dumb thing'll shoot that jag outta there."

"Let me test this old CO_2 cartridge on my air rifle before we try it on your muzzleloader," he continued. "It's really old. I don't know if it still has any oomph."

Sure enough, the cartridge worked.

"Great," I said. "Now just grab another cartridge and we'll give it a whirl."

"Oops," he replied. "I guess that was kinda dumb. That was the only cartridge I had left."

We ran to the store, picked up more cartridges, and we were all set. We screwed the gizmo on the nipple and … nothing happened.

"Figures!" Jim stormed. "You can't trust anything made these days! I don't know why manufacturers even bother! Just trying to make a buck, I suppose."

A couple hours after I'd arrived, we were still scratching our heads. Could we pour some black powder down the nipple and shoot the jag out? I'll admit, this sounded like a stupid idea, even for us.

We were out of options.

"I guess there's one other thing we could try," I announced. I walked to my truck and retrieved a synthetic ramrod with a T-handle.

"Where'd you get that?" Jim stormed.

"Uh, I bought it at the store the other day. The clerk said it's stronger than wood."

Jim scowled. His reluctance to use the new-fangled synthetic rod was evident, but we had no other choice. He snatched the piece of fiberglass from me, muttering something about, "no sanctity in this world," under his breath.

Jim unscrewed the wooden rod from the jag, screwed the synthetic ramrod tightly onto the jag, gave a firm tug on the T-handle, and like a cork popping free of a wine bottle, the ramrod came out, jag and all!

"Eureka!" I shouted. "All hail the synthetic wonder!"

With our mission accomplished, I turned to leave.

"Well, thanks, Jim. See ya tomorrow."

"Wait," he protested. "Where did you say you got that ramrod?"

"At the sporting goods store downtown. Say, you're not thinking about getting one, are you?"

"Uh, well, maybe," he stuttered. "But not a word of this to the guys at the rendezvous."

We Got a Buck!

I like old deer hunting stories. Sometimes I feel like I grew up at the tail end of a different kind of hunting culture. When I started hunting, a buck was a buck. If you got your buck, you were happy. And proud. Nobody shamed you if it was a spike buck. And you didn't need to post it on Facebook for validation.

When I first started hunting, I'd never heard of the concept of passing up a buck to let it grow bigger. If you'd have told me your buck was 170 inches, I'd have figured that's how long it was (and quick math would have made me raise an eyebrow at your 14-foot buck). It was a simpler time. And as much as I enjoy pursuing big bucks these days, sometimes I long for that bygone era when a buck was a buck and that's all that mattered.

Another thing has changed, too, and that's the family camaraderie of deer hunting. This notion isn't extinct by any means. A lot of families still hunt together, but not like they used to. Time was when after years of begging to accompany him, a boy finally got to tag along with Dad to that very first deer camp. It was a rite of passage; a milestone. When you went to deer camp, you had finally become a man. Never mind if the first "gun" you might have toted into the woods was nothing more than a stick because you weren't legally able to hunt with a rifle.

At deer camp, you might have watched your cantankerous grandpa waddle around in his old union suit. Your uncles played poker and drank whiskey. The rafters rang with laughter as stories of big bucks that got away were told and re-told. And at the supper table, you probably sat next to a cousin or your dad's brother-in-law who nobody likes. Some of these folks you never saw other than at deer camp and Christmas. But for a few days each fall, young and old, well-to-do and poor, locals and nonresidents all came together to hunt deer. A bunch of greasy, unkempt guys crammed in a bunkhouse for a week may not seem like a romantic image, yet I argue that there's a certain mystique to the old family deer camp.

It's places like these where memories are forged and hunting stories ascend to the status of family legends.

Sadly, I wasn't part of my family's most legendary story. I was a freshman in college when it happened, and although I had hunted opening weekend, I don't remember where I was when my family conducted the millpond drive Thanksgiving weekend that season. I missed a real rollercoaster of a hunt.

My dad and my brother, James, participated in the millpond drive that year. Joining them were Gary and his son, Trent. Gary is such a shirttail relative that we might not technically even be related, but he and my dad grew up together and they still get together and play cards with their wives now and then.

Gary is a sweet man; a genuinely nice guy who knows everybody. He's generous and caring. He's a great guy, but he does have one shortcoming … let's just say venison is not a regular commodity in his household. In fact, I couldn't tell you the last time he shot a deer.

As for Trent, well, let's just say he's the boy who never grew up. The Army thanked him for trying, but decided the country would be better off with him as a civilian. To his credit, he's had a lot of jobs … just none of them for very long. And let's just say, if he were to participate in a deer hunt with me, I'd prefer him to be a driver, rather than a stander. Drivers don't need to carry firearms.

I guess that's the nicest way I can describe this duo.

So Dad, James, Gary and Trent all assembled for the millpond drive. (See The Millpond Buck on Page 34 for more information on how this drive works). Lo and behold, the drivers rousted a small buck and proceeded to let lead fly as the deer bounded across the marsh. Gary got a few shots off. Trent was too entangled in his rifle sling to shoot. It was probably better for everyone that way.

The buck didn't go down, which was too bad because all morning Gary had been talking about a technique he had learned for removing the anus when field dressing a deer. He'd even brought along a corncob, which he claims is the key to the whole system. He was plenty excited to show the rest of the group how slick this little trick was. Maybe a little too excited.

No, the buck didn't seem hit, but the hunters followed up on the shots anyway and discovered a little bit of blood. So they took up the buck's tracks in the snow. The buck crossed a road, where it scooted across picked cornfields. A 10-acre patch of woods a half-mile distant was the logical hiding place for the mildly wounded deer, the group reasoned, and as luck would have it, Gary knew the landowner.

The crew swung into the landowner's domicile, related the tale of the wounded buck and got the green light to go after it.

But the hunters soon learned they weren't the only ones interested in hunting that woodlot. In fact, four guys were already hunting the property. It was midday, and they were at their deer shack. They weren't too happy when Dad, Gary and the boys pulled up.

Dad and Gary explained that they had wounded a buck and they thought it was lying low in the woods. They'd gotten permission from the landowner to go after it.

I'm sure if I were in the other hunters' boots, I wouldn't have been overly excited to see another group of guys show up, either. So the guys in the shack laced up their boots and decided to go along on this drive. The matter of which party got to keep the buck was not discussed up front, but I would imagine in their eyes it was every man for himself.

Gary, Trent and two of the guys from the other party would push the woods, beginning where the deer most likely entered on the north end. The other two members of their party stood in the open on the east edge of the woods. Dad walked out into a field about 100 yards south of the woods, giving the buck an opportunity to exit the security of the woods where he could get a shot at it. James posted outside the southwest corner where he could see both to the south and west.

There was certainly tension between the hunters. The four-man party obviously wasn't keen on "their" woods being driven. James was only 15 at the time and asked Dad how to tell if they had the right buck if a buck exited the woods.

"If a buck runs out," Dad said, "shoot it."

The drive got underway, and before the drivers had even reached the halfway point, a buck squirted out the east side of the woods and out into the open. A hailstorm of lead greeted the fleeing deer. Two of the standers from the other party shot, as did Dad. The buck was heading south, and as it passed the southern edge of the woods, James got a look at it, too.

The buck bounded across the open field, literally running for its life.

At 15 years old, James didn't have any experience shooting at running deer. But he had two things going for him. For one thing, he'd grown up in a duck hunting family and had fired at plenty of launched clay targets and ducks on the wing. But more importantly, James is smart. He would later graduate as salutatorian of his high school class. He's intelligent and cunning; skills he probably learned while unraveling my made-up jokes before I ever got the chance to deliver the punchline.

My brother James, aka Old Crackshot, made a 350-yard freehand shot on this running buck after drivers pushed it out of a woodlot.

As James recalled, Dad had shot four times and was holding off on his last shot in case the buck stopped or he got a better shot. The standers from the other party were shooting too, although they didn't have a good angle, as the deer was now running straight away from them. James took a couple shots. The deer was still running and by now was getting farther. He held fire and looked around. He noticed that Dad was no longer shooting. However, on his second shot, James had seen the dirt fly. That's when his scientific mind kicked into gear. All he had to do was hold a little higher and a little farther in front of the fleeing deer.

His third shot missed as well, but not by much. He recalculated, swung, squeezed the trigger and the buck cartwheeled to the ground.

No one was sure who had put the deer down, but James told Dad that when he fired his fourth shot, the deer dropped.

Both hunting parties assembled around the 5-point buck. Now it was time to figure out whose deer this was.

One of the other hunters thought he might have hit it.

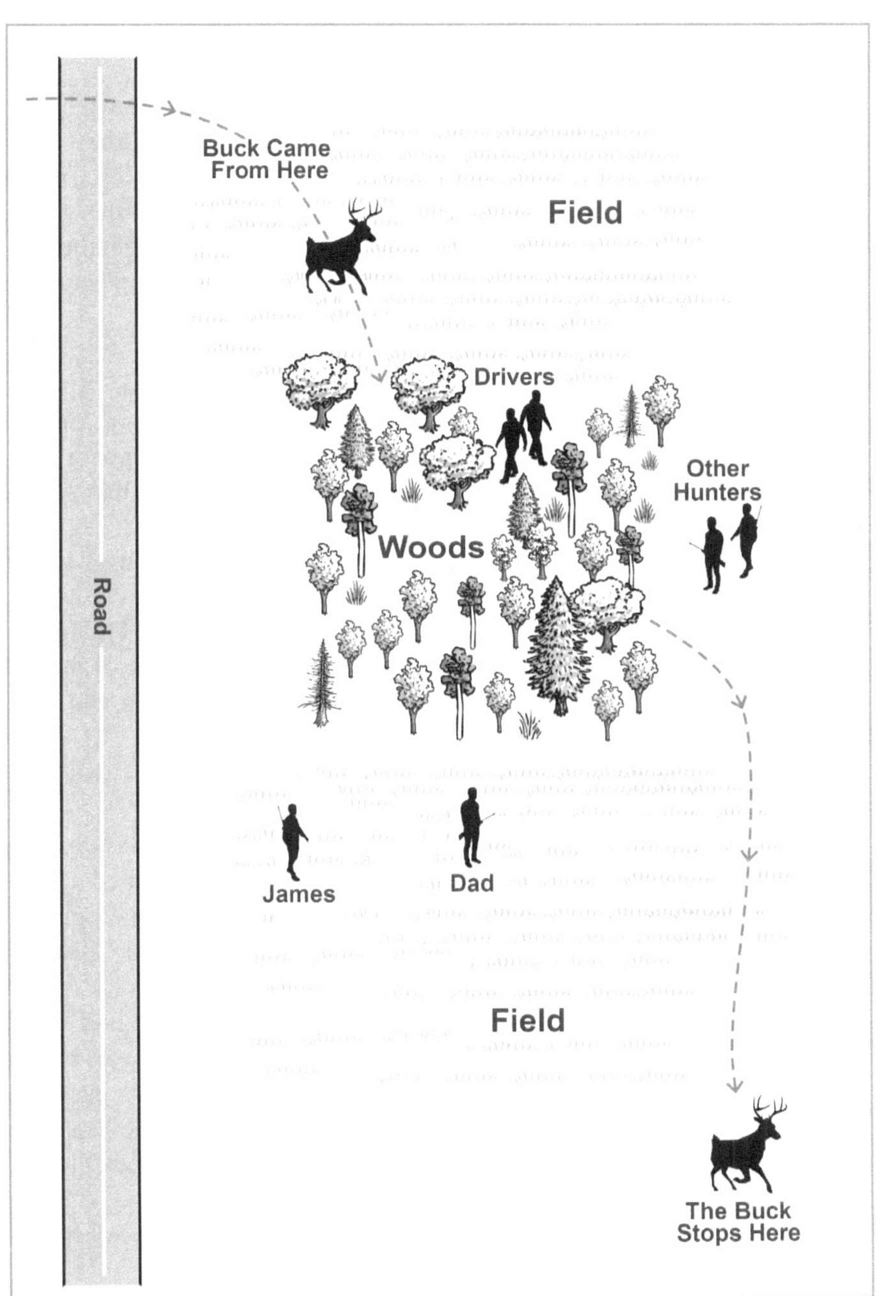

Road
Buck Came
From Here
Field
Drivers
Other
Hunters
Woods
James
Dad
Field
The Buck
Stops Here

"He says when he shot, the deer went down," Dad said, gesturing at James.

Naturally, the adults in the other party were suspicious that a teenager could have made the shot, especially considering he was the farthest from the deer! (Later, while driving along the highway parallel to the field, using the truck's odometer, Dad calculated the shot at about 350 yards). However, forensic evidence showed a single center-punched shot right through the lungs from a 90-degree angle. Only Dad or James were in position to make that shot, and Dad had stopped shooting.

It was notable that the buck exhibited no other wounds.

At this point, the other hunting party had seen enough. They'd had a buck sniped from right under their noses, from a teenager no less. And it's likely they were suspicious that the buck that Gary had fired upon a half-mile away had ever been hit. They likely suspected our guys had seen a buck run in there and just wanted a crack at it.

As the other guys walked away, James piped up. "You may want to finish the drive," he said. "I think the other buck is still in there."

To this day, he maintains there must have been two bucks. He figures the wounded deer probably was reluctant or unable to get out of its bed and when everyone bailed out the side once the shooting began, the buck probably laid low.

We'll never know if the other party did finish the drive, although it seems doubtful.

As one party walked off, disgruntled, for the other group, it was cause for celebration. Gary was most excited, because he rarely bagged a deer. James had actually shot a buck the day before and I killed one opening weekend, so our family had plenty of venison. It was decided Gary and Trent should take the deer.

If you'd seen the jubilation on Gary's face, you'd think he had killed his first deer. He shook hands all around, grinning from ear to ear. He set right in to field dressing the buck and was so caught up in his euphoria that he plum forgot to show everyone the corncob technique he had been babbling on about all morning. When it was time to drag the buck back to the truck, James latched onto a rope, and so did Gary.

At 6', 2" Gary's strides were almost twice as long as James,' but he didn't seem to realize it.

"Oh, here, Old Crackshot," Gary began. "You're doing all the work. Let me help."

James said Gary was high-tailing it so quickly with the buck in tow that it was all James could do to keep tension on his own rope. Gary whisked the deer effortlessly across the ground as James struggled to keep up.

And to this day, Gary still calls James "Old Crackshot."

With all the hoopla, Gary was late in getting home, so he asked if he could stop at my folks' house on the way home and call his wife.

"We got a buck! We got a buck! We got a buck!" he babbled over the phone to his surprised wife.

I've never heard of anyone, young or old, novice or expert hunter, so excited over a 5-point buck. It makes me smile to think that even a small buck could mean so much to a hunter.

The Trophy

In the Midwest, we're polite to a fault. If you plan on getting home at a reasonable hour, you'd better start trying to say goodbye the minute you step through your neighbor's front door. You'll need to say, "Well, I s'pose I better get going," at least a half-dozen times before you finagle your way out of a one-way conversation and can distract your host long enough to actually leave.

And we feel guilty taking the last piece of cake, even if chocolate is our sinful indulgence. Rather than steal that last piece, we just shave off a little, leaving some for the next person, who ultimately whittles it down to an even finer piece. Gradually, that ever-skinnier morsel becomes mere crumbs, but still, we leave it for the next person. In an extreme example of over-politeness, eventually the last piece grows dry, and perhaps moldy and is simply thrown out, rather than eaten. That's Midwest polite to a tee.

We've all hunted with game hogs: the greedy guys who always claim the best stand or insist they killed every bird that dropped out of a flock. They sky-blast at ducks well out of range and feel that if there are three hunters in your party, they are entitled to shoot all three limits.

As frustrating as hunting with a narcissist is, hunting with overly polite companions can be equally challenging.

For a handful of years, I hunted with a group of college friends in northwestern Wisconsin. The size of the party ebbed and flowed, blossoming to six at one point, but usually consisting of three or four. After a few years of hunting with the gang, I broke away for a chance at bigger and better things, meaning bigger bucks.

However, as deer season loomed a couple years later, I hadn't a clue where to hunt. I hadn't done any scouting and the weather was proving problematic for the area I wanted to sit. So, the day before opener, I called Ryan and sheepishly asked if I could re-join the group.

That evening was like old times. It was great to see long-lost friends and to pour all our snacks on the table and pick and choose the mix that would last us through long hours on stand. We lounged around in our long johns, drinking beer and ribbing each other over missed chances at bucks. We threw money into the big-buck pool with naive optimism, each of us convinced that we'd finally tag Bullwinkle.

Ryan boasted about his new stand. A few years earlier, Ryan and Jen had bought a house and 10 acres abutting the public land we hunt. This year, however, the neighboring farmer had given Ryan the green light to erect a tower stand on the edge of his property. From there, he could shoot on the farmer's land or onto the public. Best of all, Ryan only had to walk about 300 yards down his driveway once he walked out his back door.

Although Jen had a tag, she was watching their 3-year-old daughter, Natalie, until she could find someone to relieve her of her duties, so she wouldn't be taking the field opening morning.

That left just me and Andy. All night the two of us had been doing a little dance. He'd ask which stand I wanted, and I'd dodge the question and parry with the same. We pirouetted toe to toe all night, neither wanting to claim a stand that might have been the first choice of the other.

The night wore on, and yawns crept in. Sooner or later, we had to decide where we would hunt opening morning. It was perhaps the most delicately played game of Midwest chess I've ever been a part of. We wouldn't have stepped on the other's toes, even if we'd been dancing in clown shoes.

Finally, it was decided the stands would be assigned based on a coin toss. The only problem was, neither of us had any change, which is really just a clever precaution taken by masterfully polite Midwesterners who are aware a decision may be forced via the coin toss. By purposefully carrying no coinage, you completely eliminate any chance of hurting anyone's feelings.

Well, we had to sit somewhere, so we decided to flip a sandwich cookie. Chocolate side for the Swamp Stand, vanilla side for Ryan's old fortress.

It took another 20 minutes to figure out who should actually call it in the air.

Finally, the cookie toss put Andy in the Swamp Stand, which is the stand I actually wanted, and me in Ryan's old stand (which I later learned was the stand Andy actually wanted). We could have saved ourselves a lot of trouble if we'd just spoken our minds, but that's the way the cookie crumbles.

The following morning we all awoke early, even Ryan, who had a 2-minute walk in front of him. Andy and I, however, had to drive down the road a piece, then navigate through a tamarack and black spruce swamp in pitch darkness, bog-hopping at times through the wet areas.

We were plenty warm by the time we closed in on the little natural opening where no black spruce had found a root-hold in the sphagnum. With some words of encouragement, I left Andy behind and continued a short distance through the spruce, navigated across a small creek, then ascended about 3 feet in elevation where the forest community changed from lowland swamp to upland hardwoods. Once in the oaks, I skirted the left edge of the forest, just above the lowland brush that wrapped around a lake to keep deer from winding me. In so doing, there was also no way I could miss Ryan's stacked-log fortress.

Perhaps 15 minutes after I left Andy, a large, dark object in the wan light told me I'd found Ryan's stand. I approached cautiously and shone a headlamp inside, fearing a hibernating bear, but it was empty. I laid my rifle and small pack across the front rest, then climbed up the rear and swung a leg over like a guy crawling over a barbed-wire fence. I organized my gear and settled in.

It felt odd to sit in Ryan's stand. Or any stand for that matter. I tend to be a roamer, sometimes hunting from a climber and something just hunting on the ground. Sitting in a stand had grown to become an unfamiliar luxury.

I actually felt a little guilty sitting there. It was Ryan's stand, after all. But then, he'd picked his own poison. He'd have a short walk to an enclosed, heated stand. If he shot a deer on the public, it would be a short drag. If he shot it in the private field, he could drive a truck right to it. If, heaven forbid, Andy or I shot something, we had a long, swampy drag ahead of us!

Gradually, the sky went from inky black to a dark gray to a golden streak in the eastern sky. The first distant muffled shot announced another deer season was underway.

Nothing appeared during that magical first hour when my mind is where it should be: on deer hunting. But soon, my thoughts started to stray. Was anyone seeing anything? Certainly I'd know if Andy shot. But even though I could probably hear Ryan as well, there could be a dozen other hunters in his direction and I wouldn't know if it were him shooting.

In this era when our cell phones are as necessary to carry as our wallets, it pains me how short my attention span has grown, and soon, I retrieved my phone from my pocket.

"Seeing anything?" I texted Ryan and Andy.

Nothing for Ryan. Andy didn't respond. Good for you, Andy. Keep that phone in your pocket where it belongs.

Before too long, I decided it was time for some deer hunting shenanigans. I had killed a doe in Minnesota two days earlier and still had the empty cartridge in my pocket. I took a photo of the empty with Ryan's fortress very clearly in the background. Then I sent the photo to the boys with no explanation.

Now, I'm pretty well known for my hijinks. In fact, I have a pretty good poker face and can carry on a lie far longer than I should. Years ago, Ryan and I were grouse hunting one day and he came across a 4-point shed antler. At some point during the day I was telling another one of my stories that was probably fabricated but carried just enough truth to plant a seed of belief in Ryan's head. Finally frustrated and wanting the truth, he made me give him a straight answer. I had to swear the truth on the 4-point shed. To this day, when he wants the real scoop, he asks, "Will you 4-point shed that?" That move is the be-all, end-all play. Once the 4-point shed card is laid, I have to come clean.

Anyway, ignoring his better instincts, or perhaps just excited for someone to shoot a deer, Ryan bit on the empty cartridge photo. After all, the photo was clearly taken in his stand and only a diabolical genius would have the foresight to carry along an empty cartridge just for a gag, right?

But before I could answer, motion to my left seized my attention. As soon as I turned my head, my eyes locked onto a nice buck that had just emerged from the shoreline tamaracks and was entering the oaks. My first thought was the high rack looked like a mule deer. This deer was definitely a shooter! He was moving from left to right and if he continued on his route, which was almost a guarantee given the terrain, he would walk right in front of me, giving me a 60-yard broadside shot.

I twisted the rifle from a lying to a firing position on the high stack of logs in front of me, leaned forward and tracked the buck with my eyes. This was going to work out just perfect.

It was probably only 30 seconds from the moment I spotted the buck until he was directly in front of me. However, that was also the exact moment the sun crested the hill, and I was now staring directly into it. My eyes watered and the rear aperture of the scope looked like a green mirror. I was blinded!

The buck carried on, head down, walking swiftly through the oaks. I was in full panic mode. A minute earlier and this buck would already be on the ground. What horrid timing!

The buck was now passing me. I rested the rifle on the log and used my left hand to shield my eyes from the sun. I pivoted the rifle slightly with my shooting hand and got a washed-out, glaring view of the buck. I lined up the cross-hairs as best I could on his chest and pulled the trigger.

The buck reared up like a bronco, startled and unsure of where the shot had come from. He bolted right, running right at me. I fired again, unsure of my first shot and unwilling to let a good chance pass. I missed him that time but got off a third shot as he turned again to resume his original course, now quite aware of where the shooting was coming from. The third shot put him down, only 40 yards away.

In less than 2 minutes, I'd gone from messing around on my phone to putting a nice buck on the ground. So often it all happens so fast!

I immediately exited the stand and walked up to the wide 8-pointer. He was a beautiful buck, with a sweeping 18-inch spread, although he had unfortunately busted his right G-2. He was stocky like a mule and would later dress out at 191 pounds when we hung him at Ryan's.

I soaked in the moment and admired my buck for about a minute. And that's when an idea popped into my head: Jen! If I could get this deer out of the woods, I could watch Natalie and Jen could still hunt on opening day!

This time I took a selfie with myself and the buck in the photo and sent it off with the caption, "No bull!"

Seconds later, Ryan called.

I didn't want to take away from his hunting, but I explained to him my idea of getting the buck out ASAP so Jen could hunt. Ryan was on board. But how would we get the deer out? What about the lake? It was frozen, but would it hold? I checked. It was that in-between ice: too thin to walk on, but too thick to ram a canoe through. That left the swamp, and I wasn't savoring the idea of slogging through with a deer in tow. Another possibility was to drag it through the oak woods and get picked up at another road. It would be better walking, but we were looking at a drag north of the one-mile mark. I decided to go that route. I'd drag it out, the guys could hunt a while and when I was close to the road, Ryan would drive around and pick me up. Andy had been strangely silent in the whole matter, even though he must have known it was me shooting. Later we learned the "Boltless Dribbler" was phone-less this time.

I had dragged the buck a grand total of a hundred yards before I had decided there was no way I was dragging this buck a mile by myself. I called Ryan.

Thanks to Ryan's ingenuity, we were able to easily transport this 191-pound 8-pointer across the lake in time to give Jen a chance to hunt that afternoon.

"Hold on," he said. "Get him down to the lake and give me a half-hour."

Ha! A half-hour? To drag the buck 200 yards? Cake!

Well, I was still huffing and puffing back at Ryan's stand with the buck almost to the water when I heard a most unusual sound. My first thought was it sounded like a snowplow scraping a road, except the sound was too loud and the road was too far away. I was honestly perplexed, although I probably shouldn't have been. I turned my gaze across the lake and soon saw movement. What the heck was it?

It was Ryan in a small, motor-powered boat, slowly ramming his way across the frozen lake! I wanted to take off my hat and twirl it in the air!

For years an old 12-foot aluminum rowboat had been stashed at the edge of the lake. A mucky trail led from a parking area to the water. You had to traverse 100 yards of swamp to reach the water. In dry years, you could make it in tennis shoes if you wanted, but in wet years you were looking at knee-deep swamp ooze. Small chunks of plywood had been laid out in places to keep you from sinking into the swampy abyss.

Ryan, bless his soul, had thrown his 8-horse motor and a gas tank into his ice fishing sled and dragged them through the swamp. The 8-horse had plenty of snort to ram the boat through an inch and a half of ice.

A nice buck makes for great memories, but good friends are the real trophies. Here, the author poses with Ryan and Andy. Jen took the photo.

If I was excited to see the buck, I was doubly so to see a motorboat coming my way. This would save hours of toil!

I dragged the buck the rest of the way to the water and retrieved my gear from the stand.

I beamed as I grabbed the bow of the boat to haul it up to shore.

"Man, am I glad to see you!" I exclaimed.

"Nice buck," Ryan replied.

I gave him a quick rundown of what had happened, then we loaded the buck into the boat and made for the opposite shore. Back on the other side, the 100-yard drag to Ryan's truck was a breeze with the deer in a sled and two people on the rope.

We were back at the house well before lunchtime.

Ryan, Jen, Natalie and I ate lunch. Andy stayed in the woods. He came looking for me around noon and found the gut pile, which confirmed what he already knew. He returned to his stand and we didn't see him until after dark.

Ryan went back to his comfy tower stand, and Jen sat in a stand on their property right behind the house for the last hour of daylight.

Being in the house with a preoccupied 3-year-old gave me time to

124

reflect. It had been a whirlwind of a day. I went from no deer sightings to a buck on the ground in just minutes. I felt a little guilty. The 8-pointer was bigger than any Ryan had ever killed from his stand in years of sitting there. And although Ryan passed on the stand, the buck should have been Andy's. After all, that stand was his first choice, and I really wanted the swamp stand.

Even so, neither of the guys were jealous. I'm sure they both felt a tinge of jealousy. Who wouldn't? But they were genuinely happy for me.

The buck was nice. But there was so much more to it than a dead deer. Having friends who sacrifice their own hunting to help you, who are too polite to even admit when they want something and would do anything for you if you just asked – that's the real trophy.

The Antlerless Hunt

Antlerless deer hunts bring out the best in hunters. The hunts center on the most altruistic reasons for hunting deer: procuring venison and camaraderie. Absent are any notions of greed over shooting the biggest buck or other negative actions associated with hunting. Antlerless hunting, simply put, is deer hunting at its best.

This idea was driven home to me on a four-day antlerless hunt held many years ago in Wisconsin. Myself and three of my college buddies decided to hunt a river backwater that we hoped would receive little hunting pressure. It didn't matter that one of us had just returned from Alaska or that one was running on little sleep because he worked second shift; the four of us simply love to hunt deer, and we were all wide awake and ready to go when we rendezvoused at 4:30 a.m.

Right away it was apparent it would be a unique hunt. The wind was howling, which makes hunting difficult enough, as deer are often reluctant to move in windy conditions. However, our hunt would be extra difficult, as we had to canoe to our hunting spot through the blustery winds. With three guys in one canoe and another in a smaller canoe, we made it to the island without incident.

We exited our canoes and hiked into the woods. The night was so dark that when any of my companions stopped moving, he was lost in the night. After a short walk, Ryan stopped.

"This is where we'll put you," he explained to Andy.

Andy had never shot a deer before, and we all hoped that the first spot would be the best one. With directions on where the rest of us would be and a few encouraging words, we left him.

I was the next to be dropped off. I wasn't far from Andy – perhaps 100 yards or so. None of us, for that matter, would be far apart. The plan was to string out so we could intercept deer walking east and west. As Ryan and Chico walked off into the darkness, I saw them shine their flashlight in the air. They hadn't turned it on before, and I assumed they turned it on to show me where they were going.

With Ryan and Chico gone, I was left alone with my thoughts. It was 5:56 a.m. It would be more than an hour until legal shooting time. I leaned

Chico canoes out his doe fawn in a solo canoe.

against a large white oak and tried to stay out of the wind. I moved occasionally from one side of the tree to the other trying to find the spot that offered the best shelter from the unrelenting gusts. Within a half-hour I'd worn a circle around the base of the trunk. Still groggy, I buried my head inside my jacket and thought about drifting off to sleep, but I was too excited for the hunt.

It was quarter to seven before I realized why the guys had shone the flashlight in the air. A startled "putt" grabbed my attention, and as I looked skyward, I saw a hen turkey in the tree directly above me. As I looked around the area, I could make out four more black blobs in the limited light. It was also then that I noticed that there was snow on the ground. It had been so dark I hadn't been able to see the scattered accumulation.

Fifteen minutes until shooting time. Excitement clutched me as I loaded my rifle. A flock of wood ducks buzzed by. It was already a memorable hunt.

The first shot of the season rang out behind me. I knew it wasn't someone from my bunch, but I excitedly turned in the shot's direction, thinking maybe a deer would come running, but I saw nothing.

My eyes swiveled back and forth as I waited, not knowing which direction a deer might come from, if at all. I longed to find out if the other guys had seen anything, but I decided that the lack of shooting was a silent indication that on one had seen a deer.

At 8:09 a.m., a shot came from my right. Then another a few seconds later. It sounded like an initial shot, followed by a killing shot. At least I hoped so. I knew either Ryan or Chico had shot, and I could hardly contain my excitement! I tried to guess in my mind who had shot, but I knew I'd have to wait. The plan was to wait 10 minutes after a shot before we met up.

But so much for the plan. Andy was coming my way, and we quickly headed toward Ryan and Chico. Ryan had told Andy over the radio that Chico had killed a deer.

Soon we could see Chico and Ryan standing around a deer. To get to them we had to cross a small ditch.

As we tried to find a crossing point, a deer jumped up and ran straight away from us. We quietly pursued it, and after about 50 yards it ran back toward us. It stopped broadside at about 70 yards, right in the open. Andy dropped to one knee and shouldered his rifle. He was directly between me and the deer, so I couldn't pull up my gun. The deer stood frozen, staring at us. Andy was motionless as well as he looked at the deer through the scope. I could only stand and watch the drama unfold. After a few seconds, the deer took off. It was running through the woods and didn't present a shot. Seconds later, a large buck with a wide, sweeping rack and lots of points sprinted after the doe. Never in my life have I seen an animal run that fast.

Andy and I stared in disbelief. It was a sight I know I'll never forget.

Andy was disappointed that he hadn't shot the doe and wished he could have the opportunity back. I guarantee that I wanted him to have that opportunity back twice as much as he ever will, but such is deer hunting.

We joined Chico and Ryan and congratulated Chico on a job well done. He'd shot a doe fawn. Of course, we ribbed him a little because the deer was pretty small, but each one of us would have shot that deer given the same chance, and we were happy he'd shot it. It was meat for the table made even more special by the bonds of friends hunting deer.

We took pictures, dressed the deer, then carried it back to the canoes on a pole. We made some deer drives, always putting Andy in the places we hoped the deer would run. We saw several deer, but somehow or another they never gave us a shot or ran in the direction we hoped they would.

By that time it was well after noon. We canoed back to our vehicles,

Andy, myself, Chico and Ryan pose with Chico's deer on opening morning of a four-day antlerless-only hunt. Doe hunts bring out the best in hunters.

registered the deer and ate a late lunch. Chico called it a day. He'd been in Alaska for months and had spent little time with his girlfriend, so we let it slide. The rest of us headed back out.

It was a quiet afternoon sit for me. By now the lack of sleep was catching up to me and I fought to stay awake. I passed the time without seeing a deer.

Just as I stepped out from under the red oak I'd called my stand, I heard a distant shot. It was so windy that I couldn't tell which direction it had come from. When I didn't see Andy on his stand, I became confused. Remembering that I now carried a radio, I asked Ryan where Andy was. Ryan said that Andy was with him.

"Did you shoot?" I asked Ryan.

"Yes."

"Did you get one?"

"I think I might have."

That was all I needed to hear. Ryan is an expert marksman and I hurried to where he'd taken a stand in a deadfall.

It was now dusk and past shooting hours. We had to hurry our search to find the deer to utilize the light that remained.

Ryan quickly related the story of how he'd watched six or seven deer, including a 6-pointer "eating acorns like pigs." Just minutes before season closed, he was able to determine for sure that one of the deer that separated from the herd had no antlers. He found the deer in his scope and the .30-30 roared.

Ryan gave us excellent directions to where the deer had been standing when he fired. We were only 70 yards from Ryan, but it was so windy that we needed the radios to maintain contact. Just as we reached the spot Ryan sent us, I noticed a light-colored spot on the ground 30 yards away. I raced over to it and found Ryan's doe.

"You got it, Ryan!" I yelled back to him.

He and Andy raced over to admire Ryan's buck fawn.

We repeated the process we'd performed on Chico's deer, then canoed the deer back to the trucks. I must say, you have not truly hunted until you've experienced canoeing with a deer in the moonlight.

Friends came and went, pitching in on the butchering intermittently the following day, and by that night, both deer were completely taken care of.

Two nights later we threw a feast with fresh vegetables, elk shot in Idaho the week before, halibut caught in Alaska the previous summer, rice and of course, fresh deer heart. As we sat down to enjoy the meal, I was surrounded by good food, good friends and good memories.

Deer Hunters' Almanac 2004

Small Bucks

The call from Opie at 11 a.m. the day before the 2018 Wisconsin gun-deer season was not what I wanted to hear. For the fourth straight year, Opie had driven several hours up north to hunt public land with me. His plan was to hit the woods and make sure his spot from last year still looked productive this year. Definitely last-minute scouting and certainly not ideal, but it was the best he could do. But his call told a different story.

High water had flooded the swamp. Worse, a November blast had frozen it. It was that in-between ice – you could stand on it for a second, but then you broke through. In essence, our deer stands were unreachable.

I was scrambling to wrap up my own projects so I could afford to hunt a few days and didn't have time to scout with Opie. But the situation was dire and I had no choice but to meet up with him. With opening morning only 18 hours away, all our plans went out the window. We had to put together a whole new plan in a hurry.

There was a way to bypass the swamp … but it would require us to cross open water. However, I reasoned this ice may be thicker. The decay of plants in the swamp produces heat and unsafe ice. We'd have to "bobsled" in my canoe across the ice covering the standing water. With our ice creepers on to provide purchase on the glare ice, we rested both hands on the canoe's gunwales, then ran hunched over across the ice like bobsledders. At the first sign of cracking, we would pile into the canoe. It's something I've done many times before on duck and deer hunts. Maybe not the safest idea, true, but it has always worked for me. Worst-case scenario, the water was shallow and the bottom hard, but staying on top of the ice was the plan.

As I'd hoped, the ice over open water was thicker than in the swamp. There was a good 3 inches. Heck, it was even enough to walk on, but the canoe would be good insurance for any weak spots. With a little effort, and a lot of slipping and sliding, we made it around the wet swamp and reached hard ground.

Now we needed to find new stand sites. I'd grouse hunted the area a bit years ago and had some idea of where to go, but Opie had never set foot in these woods. I decided to head for a natural forest clearing I remembered stumbling upon.

The forest consisted of mature aspen, pocked with groves of super-canopy white pines. From the swamp below where we intended to hunt, hills thrust up suddenly, making for some rugged terrain by Wisconsin standards.

As we neared the clearing, a series of rubs and scrapes caught Opie's eye. A couple trails came together there, and Opie reasoned a buck might come cruising down the scrape line. It was a long hike back to the scrape line, so rather than carry his climber and get all sweated up in the dark, he vowed to just stand on the ground near the trail intersection opening morning.

Opie is a planner, and now, with one whole hour of daylight to spare the day before deer season, he had his new opening morning plan.

As I went to bed that night, I still wasn't sure what I was going to do. I decided to play it by ear, which is my style and the exact opposite of Opie's style. Winging it would absolutely kill him. Maybe that's why I decided to wing it.

I jolted out of bed at the ringing alarm the following morning and instantly, a plan formed in my head. I would walk in with Opie halfway to his spot, then stay behind and overlook a promising ridge for a couple hours. Then I'd still-hunt my way to pick up our trail cameras, which we hadn't had a chance to check. I'd skirt the swamp to get them. I'd still-hunt the rest of the day or stop and hunt if I found a spot I liked. It wasn't a solid plan for Opie, but it suited me just fine.

The following morning, we bobsledded across the ice with minimal amounts of gear. If anything, the ice had grown thicker overnight. We easily followed our tracks from the afternoon before in the dusting of snow that had fallen earlier in the week. I stopped at my predetermined ridge and we wished each other luck on our opening day audible plan.

Opie's footfalls faded quickly, and seconds later, I was enveloped in darkness. My mind drifted like it always does to past deer openers. Bucks tagged. Bucks missed. Hunting companions. Places where I've watched the sun rise on this most sacred of days in Wisconsin. There were a lot of years where I had a stand waiting for me on private land. It sure took the guesswork out of the hunt. And there was one year where another hunter and I arrived at the same spot at the same time opening morning on public land. He had a ladder stand set up and waiting for him, while I'd brought a climber. Even though I'd hunted that spot a couple years already with the climber, I let him have it. It would be nice to have a solid gameplan for

My opening morning buck sported 5-inch spikes. Minutes after I shot him a much nicer 8-pointer appeared. Oh well!

today, but I didn't mind. I don't feel the pressure to get a deer like I used to.

Gradually, grayness replaced the inky blackness and soon, my phone showed shooting time. My eyes peered down the ridge below me, looking for any sign of movement while my ears strained to pick up the sound of crunching leaves. But there was nothing. And then boom!

A rifle roared not too far away. I looked at my phone … it wasn't even 7:00 yet. Was it Opie? It had to be!

I waited for Opie to text me. A couple minutes later it came: "Buck down!"

Things unfolded exactly as Opie had hoped. A spike buck came walking down the trail intent on checking scrapes and Opie was in perfect position to ambush the deer. Even though it was only a spike, the deer dressed out at 140 pounds – clearly not a yearling.

I was tickled. Mere hours before the hunt, we had absolutely no idea we'd be hunting in this area, and now Opie had a buck on the ground. True, it wasn't a giant, but it was a sweet reward for public land hunting in northern Wisconsin.

Of course, Opie declined help with his deer. It was still early, after all. "Go hunt," he said. So I put my plan into action. Now in the full light of morning, I slowly worked down the ridge in the direction of our trail cameras. I hadn't gone far when I spied another ridge that looked irresistible. I just had to find out what was on top!

I clambered up a heavy deer trail and as soon as I crested the ridge, I heard the unmistakable crashing of deer running. Oops! Well, at least they were here.

Slowly, quietly, I worked my way along the edge of the ridge. I'd only gone a couple hundred yards when I heard crunching in the leaves below me. I froze. Something was coming toward me at the bottom of the ravine I was overlooking. From my vantage point, I had a commanding view of the ravine. And best of all, between the elevation difference and the wind direction, there was no chance whatever was coming would wind me.

Seconds later a doe snuck into view. I scrutinized her heavily, but no matter how hard my eyes strained through my binoculars, I couldn't grow antlers on her head. As she passed below me, I heard another deer behind her. The moment of truth! Would it be her fawn … or a buck?

Sure enough, here it came. The fawn-or-buck conundrum was not immediately solved. The deer was not large by any means, and given my position high above it, my depth perception was off. But based on body behavior and size, I thought it was a buck. Still, it was not easy to see antlers. I stared as the mystery deer walked slowly behind the doe. Finally, it entered my best shooting lane. But rather than shoot it as it stepped into the clear, I used the opening to confirm that, yes, there was something on its head, and, yes, his spike antlers were the legally mandated 3 inches tall … but not by a lot!

The buck was now getting back into the brush. I'd taken a couple steps to get around some brush between myself and the deer and was preparing for a freehand shot. I fired and the doe ran off, but the buck froze. Not knowing if I'd hit it or not, I shot again. And a third time. Still, the buck stood still.

By now I could feel my phone vibrating in my pocket. I was sure it was Opie.

The buck remained where it was, unsure of what was going on and giving no visible signs of a hit. I figured my shooting was not great in the freehand position, so I gambled and took a few quiet steps to another tree for a rest. All the while, the buck stood below me, seemingly oblivious to

When the weather threw us a curveball on opening day of deer season, Opie and I called an audible and we each killed a spike buck. Despite their small size, these bucks really put the fun back into hunting

what was happening. At the fourth shot, from a solid rest, the buck took off. I listened as it crashed through the brush until the sounds faded away.

I checked my phone. Opie was quite concerned now. I'd just shot four times … what the heck was going on? Before I could respond, I heard more footsteps in the leaves. Suddenly, an 8-pointer appeared, only half as far as the other deer had been! I honestly didn't know if I'd hit the spike, but I had to assume I did, so the 8-pointer got a pass. He did spot me as he tried to climb my ridge, and although I'd just fired a rifle four times, he didn't seem too concerned (maybe he had witnessed my lackluster shooting?) and slowly ambled off in the direction the doe had gone.

After 15 minutes, I decided to look for my buck. Thankfully, there was snow, which helped me find his tracks and eventually a blood trail. He hadn't gone far before piling up. Not surprisingly, there was only one bullet hole in him. I really have to practice my freehand shooting!

I looked at my phone. It was 8:30. I texted Opie that we were tagged out on opening morning!

My 5-inch spike was not the biggest buck I've ever killed. But he's certainly one of the most memorable. Opie and I had been thrown a curve by Mother Nature. We had scrambled to put a plan together and it worked better than we could have expected. Of course it would have been better if we'd both killed 10-pointers, but honestly, we didn't care.

When I started deer hunting, you shot the first buck you saw. Then, "rules" were put in place on the private land where I hunted that a buck had to be of a certain size to kill. It certainly improved the size of the bucks, but inevitably, someone would shoot one on the last day that was borderline and it put a rift between everyone. I felt like I was constantly watching over my shoulder and trying to please everyone else, rather than hunting for myself. It sure took the fun out of it. That's when I made the decision to leave the private hunting I enjoyed and hunt up north on public land and I have no regrets. It hasn't been easy, but I feel like I've earned every deer I've shot. And it has put the "hunt" back in deer hunting for me. I do like big antlers, and I actually passed up a spike opening weekend of both the 2016 and 2017 deer seasons. But with limited hunting time in 2018, I had no reservations about pulling the trigger. I have no qualms about how a person hunts, where they hunt or what they shoot, as long as the hunt is conducted fairly, ethically and legally. And ultimately that the hunter – not anyone else – is satisfied with the kill.

Opie and I have both taken some nice bucks in just the last few years. And although all have their unique stories, none have been as fun as the spikes we killed on our 2018 opening day hunt. All day long as we toiled to get those bucks out of woods and across the ice, we just laughed at our improbably good fortune. It was some of the most fun I've ever had while deer hunting. And isn't that what it's all about?

Wisconsin Outdoor News
2018

Part III
Reflections

Stressed

It had been a busy fall. He was always busy, but being busy in the fall was intolerable. There were better things to do in fall.

The busy summer season at work had dragged into October, and he felt like he couldn't afford to take the vacation days he had earned. During the evenings, he was engrossed in writing his first book – something he'd been working on for three years and absolutely had to finish by mid-November. On top of that, he was quitting his job in a month – a dream job – and the thought of leaving it and his co-workers hurt more than a little. But it was time to try something new. The new job necessitated a move five hours away from a place he had grown to love and call home. The lakes, swamps and forests he was leaving behind would always beckon him like a childhood friend who moved away, saying, "Come visit me someday." As he packed his household belongings, purposefully leaving out his hunting gear, he hoped he could.

To say he was stressed out was an understatement.

In spite of his saturated schedule, he'd found time to spend a few quiet mornings in a duck blind and get out the bow for evening sits in the tamaracks. A man had to take some time for himself once in a while to keep his sanity. But as October began to drift away like a scarlet maple leaf on an Indian summer breeze, he saw that, once again, his dream of an out-of-state big-woods deer hunt was destined to remain just that.

For years, he'd fantasized about hunting in northern Minnesota. It was big country, with millions of acres of state and national forest inhabited by moose, bears and wolves. And although the deer population was a fraction of what he was used to, the thought of seeing a thick-racked buck that could be 5 or even 10 years old would make long, deer-less hours on stand tolerable. Best of all, there was plenty of room to roam and few hunters. It really was a hunter's dream.

But always, it was just a dream.

As November loomed on the horizon like a twilight full moon, it occurred to him there is never a good time to do anything. Maybe when we've got more money, we say. Or maybe when we're married, or after the kids are out of the house. When we're retired – that's when we'll have time to do the things we want to do. But it rarely works that way. How could postponing his dream hunt another year make it any closer to reality?

These thoughts, and many others, rushed through his head one day a week before the Minnesota gun season. That's when he felt himself rise from his desk at work. His mind was clouded, and as he drifted over to his boss to ask for a couple days off, it was as if he were seeing the conversation from above; as if he were watching someone else. Words fell out of his mouth, echoing in his head and sounding far off. After a minute, he half-floated back to his desk, clutching a signed piece of paper that was his ticket out of work. He crinkled it in his hands, read it over again. It didn't seem real. But he was going hunting in Minnesota.

There was too much to accomplish at home, but what difference would a few days make? He was delighted to learn that it's hard to concentrate on the annoying things in life as you excitedly pack your truck for a North Woods deer hunt.

He was winging it, and he knew it. He had fished in the area a few times, but had never scouted for deer. A topo map purchased on the way north would be his guide.

Friday evening, after a long day's drive, he had just enough daylight to confirm that his chosen spot on the map looked promising. Deer tracks dotted the area, and he found a scrape on top of a high rise jutting up between a rock-studded river and a dry creek bed. He left his climbing stand at the base of an aspen and climbed down the rugged hill. That night, for the first time in many years, he felt that child-on-Christmas-morning pre-hunt excitement.

Morning came quickly. He stepped out of bed and grinned. The dream had ended with the ringing alarm clock. This was real.

Back up the hill he climbed in the darkness. It was nearly straight up, and at times he lunged from tree to tree for a handhold, ever mindful of his rifle muzzle. The climb was much more difficult than it had been in the daylight, and twice his feet slipped out from underneath him, planting him flat on his stomach with only his death grip on a tree keeping him from tumbling downhill into the river below. He was glad he'd left the climber in the woods the night before.

After a few minutes of arduous climbing, he stood atop the hill. Sweat moistened his brow, even though he was wearing only his long johns.

He walked slowly, carefully through the aspens and pines to the eastern slope where he'd left the climber the night before. No need to hurry, he reminded himself. No sense spooking anything bedded on top.

The climber was as he'd left it. He donned his hunting clothes, shouldered his backpack and shimmied up the aspen. By the time he pulled up his rifle, it was getting light.

Shooting time came. He smiled. He was finally here.

The silence of opening morning was deafening. Back home, the first shot would have echoed across the land when it was too dark to see. By legal shooting time, it would sound like a war zone. But it was mostly quiet here, save for the chattering of a few red squirrels and the faint whispers of sporadic, far-off gunshots.

The season was only a half-hour old when he heard a twig snap. He cocked an ear and listened. The cover was thick, and even from his perch 15 feet up the aspen, he could only see about 30 yards. Another faint crunch reached his ears. Something was definitely coming, but it was moving more quietly than any deer he'd ever heard. Whatever was moving through the brush was making a career of keeping silent. Finally, after 10 agonizing minutes, he made out a deer's ear. His heart throbbed in his ears and his mouth was parched as he shouldered the rifle. His vision through the scope was no better than with the naked eye in the brush. Was it a buck? He couldn't tell, but if it was, it wasn't very big; he'd have seen a large rack. He was no trophy hunter, but he hadn't driven seven hours to kill a spike or fork first thing opening morning.

Before he ever got a good look at it, the deer melted back into the brush as silently as it had appeared.

The deer was gone, but he was happy. He decided that seeing a deer during the first hour of season wasn't bad for a guy whose only scouting had been with a topo map.

He sat. He sat and thought about the book, about work, about the impending move. Should he back out and stay at his job? It would be easier. It's always easier to maintain the status quo. No, he was committed. The thought of leaving his co-workers and his old job twisted a knot in his stomach, but it was for the best. There would be new adventures and new places to explore.

He was surprised how quickly time passes when you're alone with your thoughts. He saw another deer – a fawn – around 11 a.m. Before he knew it, the sun began to slip down the hillside. He hadn't seen a deer for hours, but he'd done some good thinking. On the way across the hilltop, he walked right into an old, green shed antler from a 130-class buck. Maybe this was a good area after all, he thought.

The next day, he poked into the woods a little deeper to a small clearing 150 yards beyond where he'd sat opening day. It was nice to be able to see a little ways, even though the clearing was only 50 yards across. He perched on a fallen log there. It was as good a spot as any.

No deer appeared at first light, but at mid-morning, five does and fawns passed him at eye level, not 15 yards away. It was an exhilarating sight and he was pleased that the first three deer didn't notice him and the last two didn't seem to care.

By the end of the day, he still hadn't seen so much as a glint of antler, but it didn't really matter. It felt good to sit down on a log and make things right in his head.

Day 3 arrived. It was the last day of his hunt and he told himself he could only sit until noon. His intent had been to kill a mature buck, but after facing the reality of seven deer sightings in two full days of hunting, he wondered if he shouldn't shoot the first doe that walked by. As he climbed the hill that morning, he didn't know what he would do if the situation presented itself.

He returned to the fallen log where he'd seen the does and fawns. It was the first week of November and he hoped that where there were does, there would be cruising bucks.

First light came and went, and all was silent. Then, around 8:30 a.m., the drama he'd dreamed about began to unfold.

The hollow sound of thumping hooves reached his ears. His eyes darted to the north and he readied his gun. Moments later, a doe and fawn broke into the clearing, passing only 10 yards from where he stood. The deer trotted halfway across the clearing and stopped. They stared at the blaze-orange blob. Perhaps they'd never seen a human before. Curiosity won out, and the doe took a hesitant step forward to better study this oddity. The fawn followed, and soon they stood 20 yards away, perfectly broadside and unobstructed.

For a moment, he thought about shooting. His tag was good for any deer. But before he could shoulder the rifle, reasoning – clear-headed reasoning – interjected. He hadn't come here for a doe.

And then it happened. The brush rustled almost imperceptibly in the direction the deer had come from. But he'd heard it; so had the doe and fawn. Something was coming. It had to be a buck!

His eyes swiveled from the deer in front of him to the tangled undergrowth behind him. There was nothing but brush – thick, impenetrable brush – and then, after seconds of careful scrutiny, he discerned a swishing white tail. His eyes strained until they hurt, but they couldn't detect any more of the deer standing 30 yards away – just that gently twitching tail.

Now he was trapped. The two deer standing in the clearing stared at him. He couldn't move to better see the mystery deer, which remained motionless, save for that flitting tail.

"Don't you blow at me!" he pleaded with the two deer in the clearing. "I've already decided to let you walk. Don't ruin it for me now."

All three deer remained still. He felt like a pawn in a big-woods chess match, and it was the deer's move.

Seconds ticked by and nothing happened. He waited, powerless to do anything, but empowered that he was a part of it. For the first time in a long time, he felt alive.

He stared at the mystery deer; stared and hoped and waited. It was agonizing, but there was nothing he could do but wait for the deer to make a move. There was no book, no job, no move on his mind; just three deer and a hunter in an age-old North Woods drama.

Whew! The doe's unexpected snort nearly made him jump. Whew!

His mind scrambled to undo the damage the doe had done. He grabbed his grunt call and did his best to sound like another deer, but the deer in the brush wasn't buying it as it slowly faded into the thicket, keeping a constant screen of brush between itself and the hunter so desperately trying to get a look at it. The doe and fawn trotted off too, and suddenly he felt very alone. He wondered if he'd imagined the whole encounter.

And then, instead of cursing his luck, he smiled.

Deer & Deer Hunting
March 2008

Empty Spaces

I knew it was just a matter of time. For a half-hour, a doe and two fawns had been milling around my tree stand. Suddenly, as if shocked by an electric fence, they bolted downhill, passing mere yards from my elevated position. But I hadn't scared them. Another deer, then two, appeared on top of the hill, veiled by a thin wall of balsam fir. I raised my rifle to get a look at their heads. Doe and fawn. Five deer within sight at the same time. It was more deer than I'd seen all season!

It was early November and the peak of the whitetail rut. With that many deer in sight, I vowed then and there I wasn't leaving until I shot a buck or darkness chased me home.

It didn't take long after that. The doe with the single fawn also came crashing past my stand, fleeing from some yet-unseen intruder. Seconds later, the tall-tined culprit revealed himself. He trotted into view, then paused to look at the fawn, which had lagged behind its mother. I got a glance at the rack and that was enough. He would easily be one of my biggest bucks, if not the biggest. If he continued after the doe, he would waltz right into a shooting lane I had just cleared a week earlier. Deciding he was more interested in the doe than her offspring, the buck continued walking toward the opening. As he reached the edge of the lane, for some unknown reason, he broke into a trot, and then, just as my finger tightened around the trigger, he accelerated into a full-out sprint toward the doe. At the shot, all six deer bolted from sight.

I found a lot of white hair and a few drops of blood that soon petered out to nothing. Even so, I slogged around for more than two hours, hopeful to find more blood or a body. But I came up empty. I was crestfallen: at first for missing my chance at a nice buck, but as the search for him came up empty, for his welfare. My heart was broken. I only hope his wound was superficial.

I have the utmost respect for my quarry and that admiration deepens every year. But no matter how much I prepare for my hunts, sometimes things just don't go as planned. I have no sandbags to stabilize my rifle in my tree stand, and I can't always wait for a perfect day with no wind or rain to take a shot. And you never know when a cagey whitetail is going to run, screech to a stop or duck an arrow.

I am happy to say that when I pull the trigger, all my shooting practice, scouting, early-morning wake-up calls and other preparations usually are rewarded with a dead deer. But I am human. Unseen branches, emotions, nerves and flat-out bad judgment have caused me to miss.

Whenever my shot goes awry, I take it deeply personal. There's no one to blame but myself. Usually, in hindsight, I can look to one moment or one bad decision where it all went wrong. The emotional drubbing I give myself after finding that "aha" moment is the worst kind of torture. But there is no stop or rewind button. I can't go back and fix it. It is a helpless feeling and it's my burden to bear. Forever. It has made me question my marksmanship, my woodsmanship and my ability as a hunter. At times, it has even made me want to quit hunting altogether, and I know people who have left the sport because of these types of incidents. But time has a way of healing emotional wounds, if not some physical wounds as well.

Fellow hunter, don't think that because I write these words that missed or wounded deer are a habit of mine. If they were, I would surely quit hunting or strive to improve myself. It's just that I don't take poor shots lightly.

Each season, as I spend time in the woods doing what I love, I reflect on past hunts. I revel in the memories of first deer, excited hunters, great shots and antlers that honor a place on my wall. But the ones that got away are just as much a part of my hunting story, and I think of them whenever my mind starts to wander on the stand.

And whenever I peer wistfully at the empty spaces on my wall.

Deer & Deer Hunting
December 2012

Dad's Deer Gun

Dad is a duck hunter – always has been, always will be. He's never had any other hobbies and never really seems to be interested in anything else, but for two months each fall, he lives for duck hunting. For years, he spent his weekends and vacation days sloshing through the marsh with his ancient, decrepit Winchester Model 1200. My father and that shotgun were seemingly joined at the shoulder and butt plate, and it was almost with reluctance each November that he went to our spare bedroom and brought out his "deer gun."

The "deer gun" is the name my brothers and I gave his .270 Winchester rifle. We didn't know what else to call it. Deer were the only things Dad hunted with it. Everything else he hunted with his shotgun.

It was always an exciting moment for me when he uncased the rifle and laid it on the piano bench the night before opening day of deer season. The Remington 760 Gamemaster, with its 3x9 scope, shiny blued barrel and glossy Monte Carlo wood stock bore a stark contrast to his workworn shotgun, which barely retained a shred of varnish on its wood. I was fascinated with everything about that rifle, from its short, skinny barrel to the fancy checkered forearm with a black-tipped edge that always looked like a deer leg and hoof to me. And those bullets! "How could a person possibly kill a deer with those tiny bullets?" I wondered. The shotgun shells he used for hunting ducks were so much bigger.

Every year, Dad put his duck hunting on hold for a few days as he pursued antlered quarry. And although my brothers and I scrambled out to his truck to examine his buck the second he pulled into the driveway if he got one, he seemed less than thrilled. Deer hunting was more of an obligation than an enjoyable activity for him.

When I turned 12, I became Dad's new hunting partner. We hunted waterfowl as often as we could. It was a thrill for me to finally be able to hunt, after serving as a spectator on Dad's hunts for so many years.

My first deer season was a memorable one. On opening day, Dad shot a forkhorn with his "deer gun," (which by then I knew was a rifle) and I shot a beautiful 7-pointer with my shotgun the next day. It was the biggest buck we'd seen in years, and Dad's biggest rack fit inside the 7-pointer's.

This Remington 760 Gamemaster, chambered in .270 Win., has been in my family for more than 40 years. My father shot this 7-pointer with it in 1984 (that's me on the left and my brother James in the middle). I've toted this rifle every year since 1993. Since then, I've killed more than 30 deer with it, plus a caribou and a moose.

Needless to say, I was hooked on deer hunting.

My Winchester Youth Model 1300 20-gauge served me well my first three years of hunting. I bagged numerous ducks, geese and pheasants with it, and a deer every year. But my brother was now old enough to hunt and he needed a gun. Besides, I was growing, so I upgraded to a 12-gauge that year for bird hunting.

I hadn't given deer hunting much thought that season. I assumed I'd hunt with a shotgun as I always had. But one day that fall, Dad showed me a classified ad for a .270 in the newspaper.

A few days later, Dad and I were looking at the rifle. It was a great gun – practically new and in great condition. We bought it on the spot. We were both excited about the new rifle. When we got home, Dad brought out his old rifle, and we examined the two guns. He asked which one I wanted, convinced, I'm sure, that I'd go for the new gun. What teenager would want a 20-year-old pump when he could have an almost-new semi-automatic? I think he was pretty surprised when I told him I wanted his old gun.

Since that day, I've carried that rifle every November, and despite thoughts of bigger calibers and heavier bullets, I know I'll shoot it for many deer seasons to come. Someday, when the gun is old and worth more to me for its memories than its use in procuring venison, I'll retire it, just as Dad has left his Model 1200 in the gun rack for nearly a decade now, while a new semi-automatic shotgun carries the load these days.

And although my favorite pastime is deer hunting, rather than duck hunting, I know, contrary to what some may think, that shooting that nice buck my first season had little to do with my passion for deer. Just as that Model 1200 made Dad a duck hunter, Dad's deer gun – *my* deer gun – made a deer hunter out of me.

Deer & Deer Hunting
December 2001

Postscript:
Since this story was written, 20 more deer seasons have passed and I've toted Dad's deer gun during every one of them. Since I began hunting with that rifle in 1993, I've shot more than 30 deer with it, plus a caribou and a moose.

Ready for a Buck

I may be the only deer hunter in the world who doesn't expect to shoot a buck on opening day. I suppose you might say that makes me a lousy hunter. Someone who has diligently scouted prior to the season, learned which bucks were present and had a good idea of their movements would put a solid opening-day plan together and would stand a reasonable chance of bringing home the venison the first time out.

But not me.

More often, the season sneaks up on me and I hastily throw my gear together the night before opener, rummaging around frantically to find stray hunting paraphernalia. Stuff is thrown haphazardly into my truck, and I'll probably spend 10 minutes digging around for loose gloves or misplaced snacks before I slam the truck door and hit the trail opening morning.

I haven't had time to scout. For that first sit, I'm banking on deer using the same old spots I always hunt. If there's any redemption for me, I hunt funnels, so the terrain and deer movements remain pretty static from year to year, but really, I'm just hoping for the best when the curtain goes up opening morning.

I stumble through the forest in the darkness, making far too much noise and sling-shotting branches into my face. The shrill clang of aluminum striking chilled aluminum shatters the tranquil forest as I clumsily affix my climber to a birch tree. Once in position, the rifle across my lap seems awkward in my hands and more than once I've completely forgotten to load it as I sat waiting for my buck.

Distracting thoughts cloud my head and few of them relate to deer hunting. I think about work and deadlines. I dwell on errands around home like stowing summer tools and toys and resurrecting my winter arsenal. Sometimes I hope a buck walks through right away so I can just get deer season over with and get on to other things.

Then there's that darn phone that somehow sneaks out of my pocket and into my ungloved hands. I text friends to see if they're seeing anything. I simply *must* check Facebook to see if people I've never even met have shot a buck yet (and of course everyone on Facebook has already tagged a giant).

The chickadees flit by, then perch just a few feet away, but I'm too busy scrolling through Facebook to notice.

Suddenly, by complete accident, I look up just in time to catch a doe sneaking through my shooting lane. I never even heard her. The phone screen goes black in my hand. My mouth goes dry and I hear my heart hammering in my ears. I've seen a thousand deer since last deer season, standing along the road or in people's yards, yet this is different. I'm hunting right now, and there's a deer in front of me. The ancient fight-or-flight hunter's response wells up within me.

In a few moments, the doe disappears into the woods, but she's caused a transformation. The phone goes back in my pocket where it belongs. My eyes scan the doe's backtrail for her male suitor. My body pivots slowly, silently. The chickadees draw near again and this time one perches on my gun barrel, accepting me as part of the landscape. Thoughts of work fade away. Work can wait. I'm hunting now.

For the first time, I notice that the golden leaves have fallen from my birch tree, even though they've been down for weeks. In fact, I notice a lot of things that my dulled senses have been too busy or too distracted to detect. The air smells fresh and crisp, like a cold Christmas tree brought into a warm house. The woodpeckers have been busy since last I sat here, probing for bugs in a rotten birch in front of me. A tall spruce has snapped in half since last season too, possibly obstructing my shot to the south.

A crazy person smile spreads across my face as I suddenly feel alive. For the first time, I'm in the moment. My thoughts are here; not at work.

What a waste it would be to shoot a buck on opening morning! Sure, it would be great to fill a tag, but what I really need is to restore something deep within me that has been dulled and repressed into the cold, dark recesses of my being, which a simple doe sighting has so quickly ushered back to the surface.

It's a wonderful thing to sit in the woods and just be. It's a pity that it takes the excuse of deer hunting to do it, but at least I'm out here now. Right now, it's me and my thoughts and I really don't care if a buck shows up. And it wasn't until that doe showed up that I realized I need quiet time in a tree more than I need venison in the freezer.

Tomorrow morning, I'll pick my way to my stand carefully, purposefully. I'll shimmy up that birch quietly. My rifle, my companion now for 30 deer seasons, will be like an old friend who you may have lost touch with, but with whom you pick up right where you left off. The phone will

I shot this 7-year-old 7-point buck after several sits on stand, by which time my head was screwed on straight and all was right in the world again.

be in my pocket. I won't care what people I've never met are shooting. I won't care about what anyone else is doing. I'll be undergoing mental therapy for the low price of a deer license and my time.

After a few days of this, when my head is clear, my soul is restored and I feel like I've put in enough time to earn it, I'll be ready to shoot a buck. I just hope he doesn't show up before I'm good and ready for him.

Deer & Deer Hunting
Summer 2021

The Death That Just Was

Spring is when I feel most alive. I'm most receptive to new ideas and my creativity bursts as I watch the snow melt, see the rivers and streams rise and watch the birds return. As much as I love winter, it bogs me down and I get stuck in a rut. There's just something about the rebirth of spring that stirs something deep within me.

Maybe for this reason, or maybe just as an excuse to get out of the house, I took a stroll on one of those March days when you're not really sure if you're in the final throes of winter or in the early stages of spring. The snow was receding and the sunny, exposed hillsides were bare, yet just a few steps into the shady woods, I sank to my knees in snow. The birds were out, but they were winter birds: eagles, chickadees, woodpeckers, ravens, even a few grouse. The honking of the spring's first geese didn't meet my ears and no robin perched on a branch above my head. Despite the warming temperatures, it must have still been winter, I reasoned.

Although I had no real destination in mind, my feet instinctively carried me down to the shore of Lake Superior. Here, in the lake's relative warmth, the ground was devoid of snow. It felt oddly satisfying to walk on bare ground after a long winter of plodding through snow. We take walking on the ground for granted most of the year, yet today it felt foreign. I can only imagine it must have felt the same way the first time an astronaut set foot on the moon.

The lakeshore is ever-changing. Driftwood washes ashore and slips back out to sea. Footprints left behind are soon swept away. Ice coating shoreline rocks, wood and vegetation slowly drips back to the lake. Waves erode the rock over eons of time. I went down to the beach, not really looking for anything, but I found something nonetheless. Today, it wasn't the ordinary pebble-sized agate or interesting piece of driftwood; it was something much more unusual. A tuft of fur caught my eye on the rocky shore. Presumably a fawn had been killed by wolves. It was an unusual sight on the beach. I've found plenty of dead deer in the woods; it just seemed odd that what was left of the carcass was lying along a rocky beach out in the open for anyone to see. Usually death is tucked away quietly in the woods.

What had happened to the fawn? Being of smaller stature than an

This deer hide, lying along the shore of Lake Superior, is all that remained of a winter-killed fawn. Although the fawn's passing seems sad and untimely, it sustained wolves or coyotes and a multitude of birds.

adult deer, had it been unable to reach enough food during the winter and starved? Or did its smaller body mass make trying to stay warm during arctic blasts impossible, and it succumbed to the elements? Did the wolves find it dead or did they run down a perfectly healthy deer? Had they killed it on the beach, cornering it against the water, or had it been dragged here as the wolves fought among themselves for the choice parts of the carcass? Or was it not wolves at all, but perhaps coyotes who had killed the deer?

I've seen death before, but the setting of this deer's final resting place is what struck me. In the foreground of the scene were a grizzled hide and two legs: all that remained of a once-living creature. In the background was a pebbly beach and a flat-calm inland sea. It was the ugliness of death juxtaposed against a beautiful beach setting. And it struck me that this maimed carcass was not an ugly, horrible thing, nor was it a thing of beauty. It just was.

Some people hate wolves. Some people love them. Wolves are neither good nor bad. They are simply a part of the landscape. The fawn had fed them.

I'm often amused by human hypocrisy in the way we perceive certain animals. Fishermen don't like mergansers because they eat too many fish. But nobody hates loons or eagles.

The whitewash on the rocks beneath the strewn deer hair told me the wolves weren't the only ones to benefit from the fawn's death. Ravens, crows or maybe even gulls had fed on the carcass. And as I stood and contemplated what I was seeing, I heard the chattering cry of an eagle, which I had spotted earlier, sitting in its nest just a few hundred yards away. No doubt the eagle had found this carcass as well.

In our civilized lives, we try to assign human opinions to everything. Too many wolves are bad. More deer are good. More moose are good. But too many deer in moose territory are bad.

The concept of good and bad are human ideas. They have purpose when assigned to Batman and the Joker. But they are foreign concepts in nature. Humans try to make everything black and white, when in reality, the environment is a complex, interconnected web. Everything relies on everything else. Like a puzzle, all the pieces must be in place to appreciate it fully.

It's easy to attach human emotions to the dead deer, and of course I felt a tinge of sadness for the fawn. Gone too soon, possibly, never given the chance to produce its own fawn or grow its first set of antlers, depending on its gender. But it had fulfilled a role, and if the eagles and ravens and crows could feel emotion, I'm sure they'd be grateful. But to them the fawn was just food.

As I walked home, I thought of my own foolish ideas. Did it really matter if it felt like a wintry March day or a spring March day? Or that it was March at all? We arbitrarily set seasons and adjust our clocks an hour. Nature has its seasons, to be sure, but I've seen snow on tulips and I've stood on 18 inches of ice in shirtsleeves. I think these are subtle reminders that no matter what our calendar says, nature is still in charge. And despite my feeling that it had been a good walk, maybe it was neither a good walk, nor a bad walk. It just was.

Tragedy

We weren't planning to deer hunt. It was Thanksgiving weekend, late in the Wisconsin deer season. My brothers and I were back home for the holiday weekend, which usually consists of a lot of eating, loafing around, playing cards and more eating.

Dad went to get the mail. Dale, the black Lab, ran outside for a little exercise. As Dad was walking back across the road to the driveway, he called over to Dale, who was at the far edge of the lawn, looking alert. Just then, a big buck ran across the road! It trotted out into the neighbor's cornfield, heading away from the house.

Dad quickly rounded up Dale and rushed inside to tell the news. We quickly decided to execute a drive.

On the southern edge of my parents' yard is a farm field. The southern edge of the field abuts public hunting land, and that's where the big buck was heading.

Dad, my brother James and I donned our blaze orange and headed out the door. James and I spent a lot of our childhood roaming around on the DNR land and I felt like I knew it pretty well. I knew a pinch point where the buck was likely to travel. If we got in position correctly, we might just get a crack at him!

I volunteered to be the driver because I knew the lay of the land and plus, I'd already filled my buck tag. The area that the buck ran into started out as a dense, boggy tamarack swamp. It was thick, and with the trees tightly spaced, it would be hard to see a deer in there. However, the swamp wasn't very big. As you move south, the tamaracks give way to some blackberry briers and then there is a narrow swath of alders not more than 20 yards wide. On either side is open marsh grass. The narrow alders run maybe 50 yards and then open up into an oak forest, which again, is surrounded by open grass.

My bet was that buck would be holed up somewhere in the tamaracks. If someone stood along that alder funnel, they should get a close shot.

The three of us began walking through the yard in our blaze orange. At the same time, a pair of deer hunters was just leaving the oak woods and walking to their truck parked at the bend in the road a half-mile away.

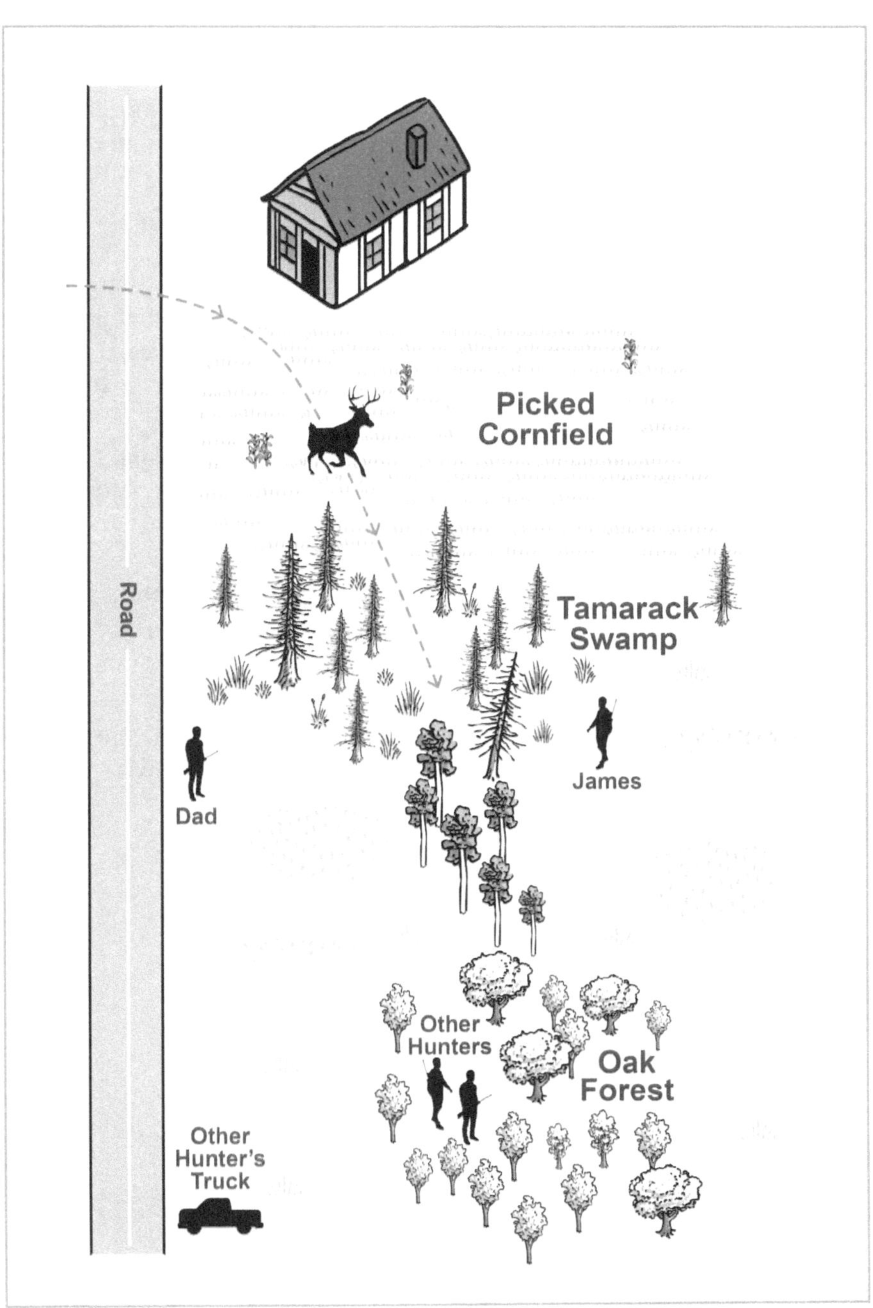

Road
Picked
Cornfield
Tamarack
Swamp
Dad
James
Other
Hunters
Oak
Forest
Other
Hunter's
Truck

They alertly realized that a drive was about to take place and did a quick about-face back to the woods.

I instructed Dad to walk down the road, then cut in just a short distance to the east and stand along that funnel between the tamaracks and the oaks. James would head to the south edge of the oak woods, loop around to the east and cover the eastern edge, in case the buck ran out the other side. However, we expected the buck to go to Dad.

I entered the tamaracks and began zigzagging my way along, doing my best to roust the deer as a lone driver. I hadn't gone far before a shot rang out. Excitement pulsed through me. It worked! However, there was one nagging thought ... that shot seemed farther away than it should have.

I continued on. Gradually, the tamaracks thinned out and gave way to alders. As I reached the narrows, I saw Dad, standing along the road. He waved me over, I assumed, to look at his buck, but the expression on his face said otherwise.

Dad filled me in on the details. As he walked down the road, he thought perhaps the buck would scoot out the side of the swamp and head west, toward the road, so he stood along the road to cut it off. Unfortunately, the buck ran right down the alder funnel, just like I expected. It ran into the oaks where the other hunting party was waiting.

As James slogged back to us, he passed the hunters and congratulated them as they set to work field dressing the 140-class 10-pointer.

In Another Year

Our hunting party gathered around Jack's buck. It was his second deer, or maybe his third. I can't remember. The buck was a yearling, but it sported an honest-to-God 9-point rack. It was Jack's biggest buck, and as a 9-pointer, it carried more points than any buck anyone in my family had shot. Sure, we'd killed some older, heavier bucks, but never anything more than an 8-pointer. But sadly, I knew what was coming, and sure enough, it came.

"That would have been a real nice buck in another year," the landowner's uncle piped up. "Too bad," he said as he shook his head and walked back to his stand, offering no congratulations or help in dragging the buck.

"In another year." The words stung me. Maybe Jack didn't care; he was too young and naïve, but those words made my blood boil.

How dare anyone degrade another hunter's deer, especially when that hunter is just a teenager! In another year? In another year, this buck might be lying dead along some highway. In another year it could be food for coyotes, having succumbed to a tough winter. In another year this deer could be miles away. Sure, it could be an excellent buck if allowed to mature, but banking on it carries no F.D.I.C. insurance.

There are no certainties in life, and especially in deer hunting. By next year, we might not have permission to hunt this land. Who knows, maybe the land will even be sold and subdivided. Heck, I can't even bear the thought of it, but what if one of us suffers a debilitating injury that keeps us out of the woods for the season ... or forever?

But here we stand around a young man's buck and I can't even feel happy for him. In fact, I'm embarrassed. Why? What did Jack do wrong?

He watched the buck cross an overgrown pasture. Then he – a product of a generation that grew up with e-mail, instant messaging and high-speed Internet – had the patience to wait for the deer to approach to within 30 yards, stop, and turn broadside before making a perfect shot. He even gutted the deer by himself for the first time.

What's so wrong about that? Nothing, and I'm proud of his patience and skill. There's no need to defend him against someone who obviously has no regard for anyone else's opinion ... and who has killed more than his share of young bucks over the years. Jack's decision will result in back-straps tonight and antlers on the wall. If he'd have passed, who knows?

Jack and I each latch onto an antler while our brother, Jim, bears the rifles. That familiar weight in my hand feels good and helps me forget my anguish.

In another year, God willing, we will hunt again. We will sit long hours on stand, hunt for days on end, and if we're lucky, tag a buck or two. But tonight we'll celebrate.

Deer & Deer Hunting
Early 2000s

One for the Wall

Before I even made an offer on what was soon to be my house, I was excited to show it off. This place was it: my Taj Mahal. Situated on an acre of land, with deer trails running through the wooded back and giant living room windows facing Lake Superior across the road in the front, it was a sportsman's paradise. I couldn't wait to show my friend Opie, so we stopped in to look at the place on our way shed hunting on a rainy May morning.

"Awesome, huh?" I boasted as we peered in through those big bay windows.

Opie's response was not immediate. And it certainly didn't reflect my excitement for the soon-to-be Shead Valhalla.

"Joe, … there's a puddle on the living room floor."

With a little lens wiping of my rose-colored glasses, I saw that Opie was right. Well, no matter. Roofs can be fixed.

I didn't let a leaky roof dim my perception of the place. True, it was a foreclosure and it had sat vacant for a year. But the location! And those giant living room windows! What wasn't to love?

By the end of summer, the house was mine. First agenda: fix that leaky roof! With a crew of friends, we had the old shingles off and a new steel roof on in just a few days.

While the guys were there, I had my old, inefficient furnace removed and a high-efficiency unit installed. Now we were getting somewhere, and just in time for fall.

Of course, then there was the plumbing. The place had sat empty for months and all the minerals that ran through the pipes all those years then dried out and clogged up everything. So I got all new faucets and all new PEX plumbing. It was only a couple days' work and no big deal, really, as long as you remember that hot is cold and cold is hot on the shower faucet that my brother Jack and I somehow installed backwards.

The final surprise was in the attic. There was a half-inch of insulation. That was it. Not ideal for a house located within 100 miles of the Canadian border! But the previous owners just used it as a summer home. Seventy bags of cellulose insulation later, I was good to go. OK, lesson learned.

Foreclosures can be a lot of work. I still thought the place was a good deal and in a great location, although I certainly stuck a lot of money into it in just the first couple months. But I was out of the woods now. Heck, I even had time to shoot a buck in Minnesota, butcher it the following day, and the day after that, I shot another one on Wisconsin rifle opener. Things were coming together in my little sportsman's paradise.

There were other little projects I could have and should have done, but after those major hurdles I was burned out for a while. Besides, I had enough to do just trying to unpack boxes and bring some semblance of order to the house.

The following summer, the Fourth of July, to be exact, I got to wondering about a crack in the plaster in the living room wall. It had been there since the day I first looked at the house. Probably just a result of settling over the years, I had hoped. But it was located just downhill of the leak in the roof and deep down I knew it had something to do with that leak. A few swings of a hammer told the real story.

Just as I feared, the water wasn't just magically disappearing when it came through the leaky roof. Some obviously ran down to the floor, but some was running down to the wall. This had been going on for years and for about six feet or so the studs were completely rotten. In fact, the plaster wall may have been about the only thing holding the structure up! It was almost beyond belief!

This wasn't just something I could ignore. This had to be fixed!

A handyman acquaintance came and looked at it. I could tell he wasn't too excited about it and we were both really busy over the summer, so we agreed to revisit the project in the fall. My text to him from late September still hasn't been answered.

Well, this needed to be fixed. But between all the money I'd already stuck into the place and the urgent need to buy a newer truck before my aging vehicle failed me, I didn't have the budget to hire a contractor. Once again, I called on my brother, Jack, who had quarterbacked all the plumbing the previous fall.

Jack was intrigued by the idea of the project. He liked the challenge, but he didn't know if he could pull it off. Plus, there was the feasibility of finding time to do it. He would stew it over and get back to me, he said.

A few weeks later, he said he could do it. He could be there Nov. 7 and could stay for a week. That was great news, except for one thing: Nov. 7 was opening day of Minnesota's firearms deer season!

Ever since I started hunting in Minnesota, I've grown to love the firearms season. The Minnesota season opens two weeks earlier than the Wisconsin season, where I have always hunted, and thus, you catch more of the rut. Big bucks are running around stupid and it can be a lot of fun.

But when you're desperate for help, you've got to take what you can get, so the date was set. I hunted opening day without seeing a deer. And then it was down to work.

It seemed like a simple project: take out a length of wall and replace it. But there was more than meets the eye. We had to remove the siding. We had to remove the toilet (which was located just behind the very end of the rotten section of wall). During the demolition process, some of the bathroom tile had to be removed and some of the bathroom wall was busted.

Then came the actual wall work itself. We began by building a support system that would hold the whole place up. Then we slowly jacked it all up. With each pump of the jack handle the whole house creaked and groaned. New cracks formed in the plaster walls and old ones closed up. Not only was the wall rotten in that spot, but as a result, it was sagging as well.

With the wall braced, it was down to business. I joked that since it was hunting season, I planned to have my rifle leaning against the wall, just in case we saw a buck run through the back yard. Jack recommended I not lean anything against that rotten wall.

We rebuilt that wall, right from the concrete foundation all the way up to the new roof. It was not easy cutting out rotten sections of sill plate and pounding in a new 2x12 with a maul. I told Jack it would have been much easier to build a new house from scratch, rather than try to drive in all these new boards into an existing framework.

Luckily, it was an El Niño November and the weather was unseasonably mild, with temps in the 50s most days. We really lucked out with the weather.

All in all, the project went smoothly; there was just a lot to do. The worst part was missing my deer hunting time. Texts rolled in from friends who didn't know about my house project, asking if I was seeing any deer. It seemed everyone I know on Facebook was shooting a monster. I hoped that we could wrap up the project early and do something fun. I wanted to at least take Jack out fishing or something for a day, but we ended up working 12-hour days for the full week.

Jack left eight days later. He had to get home to his own projects. And he had taken an entire unpaid week off work, having used up all his vacation already.

I ambushed this buck on a windy, rainy morning after working for eight straight days on my house.

The next day – the second Sunday of deer season – I saw two does out my bedroom window. They were the first deer I'd seen all season. I spent that day replacing the siding. With the siding back on, I gave myself the long-awaited green light to get out hunting.

The forecast called for wind and rain the next three days. Great.

I awoke early the next day – the 10th day of the season and only my second day to hunt. It was windy already but the rain had yet to arrive. I actually thought about not going, given the weather conditions, but I quickly reminded myself that it had been absolutely killing me not to be in the woods and now, when I actually had a chance to go, I was thinking about sleeping in and staying home?

I made the long drive in the dark without seeing a deer. I found the wind wasn't as pronounced once I got in the sheltering woods and overall, conditions didn't seem too bad. But nothing materialized that morning. I got down from my stand around 10 a.m., just as the rain began. Between the noise of the wind and the falling rain, the conditions were perfect for still-hunting. I had swung a hammer for far too long while everyone else

This North Woods 10-pointer was a sweet reward for enduring a fall of house projects when I wanted to be hunting. He now adorns the wall my brother, Jack, and I built during deer season.

was out hunting. I wasn't about to let a little rain stop me. I was going to hunt all day one way or another.

My still-hunt went better than I could have imagined. I have said it many times in the re-telling of this story: I could do that same still-hunt a dozen times over and never see a deer. But on this day – this magic day – the stars aligned and I shot the biggest buck of my life. Maybe it was dumb luck. Maybe it was karma. Or maybe it was a higher power smiling down on me. Whatever it was, I will take it. After enduring my most frustrating fall ever, it was just what I needed. My friend Jon, who received almost daily reports about my house construction while he was at his deer camp, summed it up best: "Now you've got something to put on that new wall."

Deer & Deer Hunting
October 2018

Spike Buck

My eyes had fallen into bleary repetition. On opening morning, rife with adrenaline, they scanned back and forth across this forest opening like rock stars. But by the second morning, the excitement and anticipation of a new deer season had waned, and after two early wake-up calls, they were sleep-deprived and scanned listlessly like an intoxicated man's feeble efforts to follow an officer's pen from side to side. If this were a field sobriety test, my eyes were destined for the back seat of a squad car.

But as those baby blues swept across that opening for the umpteenth time, they paused for an instant on a stump that my brain didn't recall seeing on any of the previous 9,000 passes. What's even more alarming is that stumps don't move, yet this one did. Either I really needed to catch up on my sleep or this "stump" was a deer.

With painstaking caution I shouldered my rifle from my perch on a log and peered through the scope. Nope, not a stump. Definitely a deer. What's more, it was a spike buck.

For a lot of hunters, a spike buck is an easy pass. But this deer quickly threw me into a conundrum. Sure, I wanted to wait for something a little – well, a lot – bigger. Ideally, I would hold out for a nice buck. But my brain starting tussling with my heart. I had a lot to do. I was working on a project that was due in a week. Of course, I'd had two months to do it, but I hadn't started 'til a few days ago. Punching my buck tag right now would free up my schedule to take care of the stuff I really needed to accomplish.

But how foolish that all year long I dream of shooting a big buck, but I was now ready to fill my tag with a spike. I constantly reassess my previous deer hunting blunders so I can make the right moves to finally tag a giant. For weeks leading up to the season, I long for opening day. Every rub I see; every scrape I find stirs excitement in my soul. This is going to be *my* year! And now this. It comes down to me wanting to shoot a spike just so I can get back to work?

No. I just can't do that. I'll never fault anyone for shooting a small buck as long as it's done legally and it makes the hunter happy. Some of my best deer hunting memories involve small bucks. Shooting this little fella would open up my schedule ... but it wouldn't make me happy.

Here he is: my opportunity to tag out, on public land in northern Wisconsin, no less, where deer numbers have been down for close to a decade. I've tagged just two bucks here in the last decade. This buck sighting is a gift, but it's one you accept with a forced smile, knowing you'll just exchange it.

It's nice to see him. It's nice to know I'm in the place where a buck wanted to be among miles of unbroken forest. I'm glad I got to watch him and to know I was given an opportunity to be successful.

What I really wish, though, is that spike buck would have walked in front of a 14-year-old kid I knew many years ago, shivering in a box blind with dorky glasses and swimming in an oversized orange vest, trying his best to grow antlers on every doe that snuck past. Hunting alone for the first time and maybe trying to grow up or maybe even prove something, days – and then seasons – passed without an antler in sight.

Seeing that spike this morning was nice. But bagging a buck – any buck – would have meant the world to me back then.

The Worst
Deer Opener Ever

It's been said many times before: there's nothing quite like the excitement and anticipation of the deer opener. On the eve of the opener, the possibilities are endless.

As usual, I was excited for my opening-day prospects for the 2012 Minnesota deer season. I had a stand I liked. I've seen a lot of bucks from it, and it's always been a reliable producer. I might not see a buck every day; heck, there are days I don't see a deer. But I know at some point during the season, I'll probably see a buck from that spot.

That season would be my fifth year hunting that stand. I'd killed three bucks from the stand up to that point and had seen several more, including a monster on opening day of 2008 – the first time I ever sat there. Although I could have shot his doe several times over, he gave me one quick look at his rack, then did an amazing job of screening himself for a full half-hour as he tended the doe until daylight ran out.

I had every reason to believe the 2012 opener would be a good one. But things got off to an ominous start. I was perched in my climbing stand on my usual birch tree when I spotted a light bobbing toward me 20 minutes before daylight. I pulled my own headlamp out of my bag and shined the hunter to let him know I was here. The hunter then pulled the classic "I'll walk 50 yards past you and then just plop down on this log" trick. Fine. Whatever. The joys of public-land hunting.

For the five years I had hunted this spot, there had been one other party hunting the area. They had been hunting the spot first. But we had gotten along rather amicably. We rarely saw each other. Usually they hunted the first three days of the season and I never saw them again. I have deer hunted public land most of my adult life, and although I hate encountering other hunters afield, I've learned that it's reality. I have bounced around, been pushed around and have grown extremely frustrated from encounters with other hunters at times, but you have to accept the fact that that's the way it is when you don't own private land.

As I sat and waited for daylight, I wasn't thrilled at the prospect of having another hunter sitting so close, but I wasn't about to foul up my own hunt by getting down and making a disturbance with prime time approaching.

First light came and went without a deer sighting. As morning wore on, I heard not one, but two separate shots from the immediate area. Later in the afternoon, I heard another close shot.

I sat all day without seeing a single deer. When I got back to the road, I found the other party at their vehicles in high spirits. The three-man party had blossomed to seven hunters. And they had killed three bucks, including a nice 10-pointer. I'd been close enough to hear all of their shots quite clearly.

Well, that's public-land hunting. I understand that. You can't be the guy in the right spot all the time. We talked for a bit. I congratulated the hunters on their success, then got the heck out of there. I wasn't mad at them for being successful. But with three bucks being killed so close to me, and without seeing a deer all day, I was sure feeling deflated!

I headed into town for supper. I usually go to a nice tavern with good food and a lively atmosphere. I like to see people at night. It can get awful lonely truck camping by yourself in northern Minnesota for a week at a time! Tonight, however, I just wanted to be alone. I went instead to a café that I knew would be quiet. Then I could mope a little, dwell on the situation and make plans for the morning.

As expected, the small café was nearly empty. There was only one couple eating when I arrived. I sat down and ordered my food. Soon, the couple departed, and by the time my food arrived, I was alone.

I ate quietly, all the while thinking about the situation. Three bucks were dead. OK, but there were more out there. And two of them were small and I'd have passed them up anyway. Besides, it was the rut. With hormonally charged bucks running around like crazy, anything can happen. Three hunters were tagged out. They wouldn't be in the woods in the morning – unless they had doe tags. Dang! Well, I still had a lot of confidence in that spot. Yup, I would just return and hope things got better. If nothing else, if history repeated itself, the other party would probably only hunt three days and I could hunt the remainder of the season alone. It's a long season, after all.

All these thoughts ran through my head. There were other spots I could try, too. And it didn't do any good to mope. That's the reality of public land hunting. Hadn't I had days when I shot a deer and the other party shot nothing? It all evens out in the end, I suppose.

With food in me, I was feeling a little better. I was nearly done eating when the café door swung open and two men entered. I looked up, and my heart stopped. No, it wasn't the other hunting party. It was two hunters, who if my initial guess was correct, were quite far from home. The younger man appeared to be in his 50s. The other man appeared to be his father. There was nothing notable about the younger man. However, I recognized his father – or at least his jacket – instantly. The elder man wore a green-and-black plaid jacket – a jacket made famous in the Northeast by a man named Larry Benoit. The September 1970 issue of *Sports Afield* pictured Benoit on the front cover and boldly asked: "Larry Benoit – Is he the best deer hunter in America?"

If my guess was correct, I was now looking at a living legend, far from his Vermont home.

The younger man pulled off his own jacket. When I saw his T-shirt – something about the Maine state wrestling championships – there was no doubt in my mind these were the Benoits.

For the unfamiliar, the Benoits are deer trackers. Larry learned to track deer from his father, who is part Native American, and whom he credited with his tracking success. The Benoits hunt the big woods of Vermont and Maine – places with low hunting pressure and room to roam – two essentials for public-land tracking. In more recent years, they have expanded to hunt in Ontario and now, I learned, Minnesota. In the Benoit camp, the hunters don't care about antler scores. They desire large-bodied bucks field dressing at more than 200 pounds. Larry killed more than 200 bucks in his lifetime. He taught his sons to track and the family has become famous. They are the real deal. Being able to track deer in snow, let alone bare ground, and getting close enough to shoot a wise old buck is the mark of a skilled woodsman. The Benoits wouldn't have it any other way.

My supper finished, I strolled over to the Benoits' table. Indeed, it was Larry and his son, Shane. They were tickled that I recognized them so far from home. They had just arrived in town and would be deer hunting in Minnesota for the second time, they said. They had gotten one buck between them on their first hunt in the Gopher State. We talked about the local area, deer movements and hunter patterns. They had quickly deciphered where most people hunt and identified places more desirable for their style of hunting.

For 15 minutes, I got to speak with them. Larry was quite hard of hearing and didn't participate as much in the conversation, but Shane was very cordial and willing to talk deer hunting. Shane said they would be "tag-teaming," which meant one man looked at the track while the other looked for deer. He said on their way home, they had an invite to hunt in Wisconsin as well.

Talking with them was a treat I won't soon forget. We talked a little about my shed hunting, and I gave them a copy of my shed hunting book, which I happened to have in my truck. Larry told me how many sheds he had found in his lifetime of tracking, and maybe someday I'll divulge that secret.

Too soon, their food came, and I thought it best to leave them to eat. We shook hands and wished each other good luck on the hunt. They each gave me their business card. I thought about asking for autographs, but was too shy. I never thought to snap a photo, even though I had a smartphone on me.

I don't know how the Benoits fared in Minnesota that season, but I do know that the 2012 season was Larry's last. He passed away the next fall at age 89.

Although I didn't see a single deer, and learned of three bucks killed within close proximity, I guess my 2012 opening day wasn't such a bad experience after all. I got to meet a living legend; a man whose sole purpose in life was deer hunting, and who eschewed stand hunting, food plots, scents and other deer hunting gimmicks, choosing instead to hunt in the old-fashioned way of a skilled woodsman. That chance encounter meant more to me than any buck I've ever tagged.

Outdoor News
Oct. 23, 2015

Wisconsin Outdoor News
Nov. 13, 2015

No Hunting Today

They were calling it "Snowmageddon – the snowstorm to end all snowstorms."

It was all the TV stations talked about. Stock up on groceries, they said. Get your snowblowers tuned up and resurrect those shovels from the back of the garage. And most importantly, don't travel if you don't have to.

That was a laughable notion. The storm would hit the Saturday after Thanksgiving – one of the biggest travel weekends of the year. Friday afternoon, I cut short my holiday weekend with my family and made the 6-hour drive home while the roads were still bare.

As the storm became imminent, the weathermen weren't backing down. They were calling for 14 to 22 inches of heavy, wet snow … and we were right in the epicenter.

Saturday dawned overcast and windy, but no snow fell. I could have been out hunting on the 8th day of Wisconsin's 9-day rifle season, but instead, I was home, scrambling to do the repairs to my snowblower that could have been done at any point over the summer.

Around noon, the first flakes began to fall. But it was warm and the snow didn't seem to be sticking to the ground. And it wasn't coming down in the blinding blizzard the weathermen were harping about.

But flake by flake, minute by minute, it built. Soon, the storm exonerated the weathermen and their bold predictions. It was as if Mother Nature had been saving up all her fury and now, like an erupting volcano, all that pent-up rage was boiling over.

Snow cascaded down in unending white sheets, driven horizontally by a relentless east wind that sucked up moisture over Lake Superior, rolled it into snowballs and pelted the west end of the lake.

The whereabouts of a road's centerline was a guessing game. Plows couldn't keep up. The state shut down the interstate overnight as cars stacked up like hopelessly marooned dominoes.

As usual, the weathermen had been wrong. We didn't get 22 inches; we got a full 2 feet. But the snow was almost impossible to measure because the wind piled it into drifts that looked like surfing waves. City residents snowmobiled down main roads while their cars and trucks sat buried under feet of snow. The snowplows were a blessing and a curse. They cleared the roads all right – and we certainly needed it – but their wake stacked up three feet of a slushy mess against parked vehicles and onto laboriously cleared sidewalks. It would be days before the snowplows even got to the side streets.

Snowmageddon indeed!

As the snowstorm moved on and left its victims to clean up the aftermath, a thought nagged at me. Actually, it had been consuming me for a while. There was still one day of Wisconsin deer season to go, and I still had a buck tag. Heck, I hadn't hunted since opening weekend.

Although I hadn't seen many deer from my stand, the tracks in the 2 inches of snow we had opening weekend told me they were there.

Things had been slow in Minnesota, too. Minnesota's rifle season opens two weeks before Wisconsin's, and I had hunted quite a bit. But deer sightings were few. After several fruitless sits, I desperately needed a change. I finally got it in the form of a snowstorm in the waning days of the season. That snowstorm, unlike Snowmageddon, only dumped a couple inches of fresh snow – perfect for tracking. With new snow, coupled with gusty winds to conceal my noisy movements, I managed to track down an 8-point buck.

And now here I was with one day left to hunt in Wisconsin and 2 feet of snow on the ground. It would be easy. Well, getting through the snow wouldn't be. I'd have to strap on snowshoes. But I knew where to go. Those deer would be bedded in the little groves of white pines that popped up here and there among the aspens, taking what shelter they could find from the deep snow and gusty wind.

I'd be quiet on those snowshoes in the soft snow, planning a stealthy attack on my prey. Sure, the deer would hear me eventually or see my movements, but I'd get pretty close. I might get a shot straightaway, but more likely, we'd go for a little chase; the deer staying just ahead of me in the deep snow, looking back on occasion to size up their clumsy pursuer.

I'd probably catch flashes of them up ahead as they moved just as much

as needed to stay ahead of me, reluctant to expend energy. But eventually, they'd make a mistake. They'd let me get too close. Or they'd get tired of wading through belly-deep snow; their hooves punching through the soft snow while I floated over the top. In the end, if there was a buck ahead of me, I'd probably get a shot.

The snow was the undoing of that 8-pointer just 10 days earlier in Minnesota.

But today was different.

That 8-pointer had no trouble moving through 2 inches of snow. But just days later, these Wisconsin deer were digging in for a 5-month battle. Two feet of snow in November is almost unprecedented. It instantly covered their food and greatly impeded their ability to travel. To pursue deer on this day wouldn't be a hunt; it would be a slaughter. Plus, I already had a deer for the year, and I honestly didn't need more meat.

Outwardly, deer and deer hunters are bitter rivals. After all, hunters are out to kill deer. In fact, we look forward to that very experience. But what some people may fail to heed is the respect we have for our quarry. Yeah, I love hunting deer. But I also love to watch deer along the road or see them walk around city parks. And each winter, I always cut some cedar boughs and leave them in my yard for the neighborhood deer to help them along in their time of need.

Yes, each fall I try to kill a deer. But even bitter rivals like the Packers and Bears or the Yankees and Red Sox shake hands after a game. Although they're enemies on the field, at the end of the day, the players still respect each other. I guess that's what I'm saying about whitetails. In the fall, we may be rivals. But once deer season is over and the tough winter weather sets in, I'm their biggest cheerleader as I watch them struggle through winter's deep snow and bitter cold.

Yeah, I could have gone deer hunting on that snowy last day. It would have been an adventure for sure. But I don't feel good about taking advantage of something when it's at its most vulnerable. I respect deer too much for that.

Last Day

The last day of deer season has a certain temperature about it. Robust laughter emanating from a deer shack full of happy, flannel-clad hunters with their bucks hanging outside on a meatpole creates a warm feeling. By contrast, standing alone in a barren, snowy woods, clinging to the slim hope that your buck will appear in the waning seconds of the season feels cold and lonely.

I have felt both.

Whether I've killed a buck or not, it's almost inevitable that I'll be in the woods for one final sit on the last day. Although I or someone nearby probably still has a tag, I really have no intention of shooting a deer. In fact, the last deer I killed on the final day of the season was in 1992. Nope, it's more about just being out there and seeing the season off.

Being in the woods as the clock winds down is a time for reflection. If I was successful, I usually wander down to where my buck came to rest on the forest floor. I like to see the progress the wolves, coyotes, ravens, crows, eagles and woodpeckers have made on the gut pile. Sometimes it's still there – a frozen last remnant of what just days earlier had been the very lifeblood of a magnificent creature. Other times, it's completely devoured overnight.

That's the happy sort of reflection. Sometimes I kneel down next to tracks in the snow and imagine "what if?" If only he'd taken a few more steps. Or if only I hadn't made that untimely noise. Then those snowy tracks would have led to a gut pile. On rare occasions there are old, frozen drops of blood on the ground alongside a well-trod human trail. Eventually the blood becomes less frequent, and finally, the human tracks simply turn back. Those are the worst reflections, and I'm thankful that they are rare.

That final sit is a lonely one. Gone are the opening day throngs of hunters with their war-like gunfire. Gone, too, are many of the deer, and those that remain are secretive, being most active after the last hunter has left the woods for the day. Even the drivers who give it one last hurrah have quit

As the clock ticks down on the final day of the season, if you haven't filled your tag, the last sit can feel extra cold. And lonely.

the woods by early afternoon of the final day. They've got a camp to pack up and a long drive home ahead of them. No, those final few hours are quiet. And lonely.

For the record, I have never actually seen a buck on the last day of season. In my early years of hunting, when most hunters shot the first buck they saw, it seemed a miracle that a buck could survive the opening-weekend barrage. And I'll never forget when one of the members of our party killed a 3-inch spike on the 8th day of our 9-day Wisconsin gun season when I was a teenager. At the time it seemed to me like the kind of thing that should have made the local newspaper because it just didn't happen. Nowadays, with hunters often passing up young bucks, far more survive to shed their antlers. Even so, I've still never seen one on that final sit, and I've often wondered what I'd do if I saw one. Would I shoot it and be happy to fill my tag like a football team kicking a winning field goal as time expired? Or would I give the buck a pass, figuring if he had made it this far, his chances of surviving and growing a bigger rack the following year were pretty good? I'm not sure. Someday I'll have to answer that question in a hurry.

176

Perhaps my favorite part of that final vigil is thinking back to all the hunts I've had over the years. I like to think back and remember what – if anything – I killed each year, where it was and who I was with. It was a happy moment the first time I realized I didn't have enough fingers anymore to tally my deer as I recalled the years. Bucks, does and even a few fawns have made my list, and although some deer stand out more than others, they're all important and they all have a story. I fondly recall my first buck and my biggest buck, of course, but then there's the buck fawn I killed at Grandma's place the year before she sold her land. It was the only deer I ever killed there, but at least I can say I shot a deer on the land my grandparents farmed and where my dad grew up.

Then there are the friends and relatives who I've hunted with over the years. Some are gone now, some have moved on to different hunting camps and some have simply drifted away, but there are still faithful companions to rekindle memories with and new hunters to create more memories.

The settings are important, too. There was the old box blind in the cornfield where my dad sat for many years, and where I sat for a few seasons even before I could legally hunt on my own. There are favorite trees that are reliable producers. There are also bittersweet memories, like grandma's old farmstead or the beautiful oak woods where I sat several seasons before it was slicked off.

As the clock ticks down, I think back to the things I've seen on stand: the young buck with the baler twine in his antlers, the buck breeding a doe, a piebald doe, foxes, a wolf, eagles, woodpeckers and more animals than I can recall. How many chickadees have landed on my gun barrel? And if you added up all the points from all the bucks I've ever killed and divided it all out, how many points does my average buck carry?

It's a lot to contemplate. No wonder I never see a buck on the last day.

Deer & Deer Hunting
June 2019

Part IV
Bull Tales

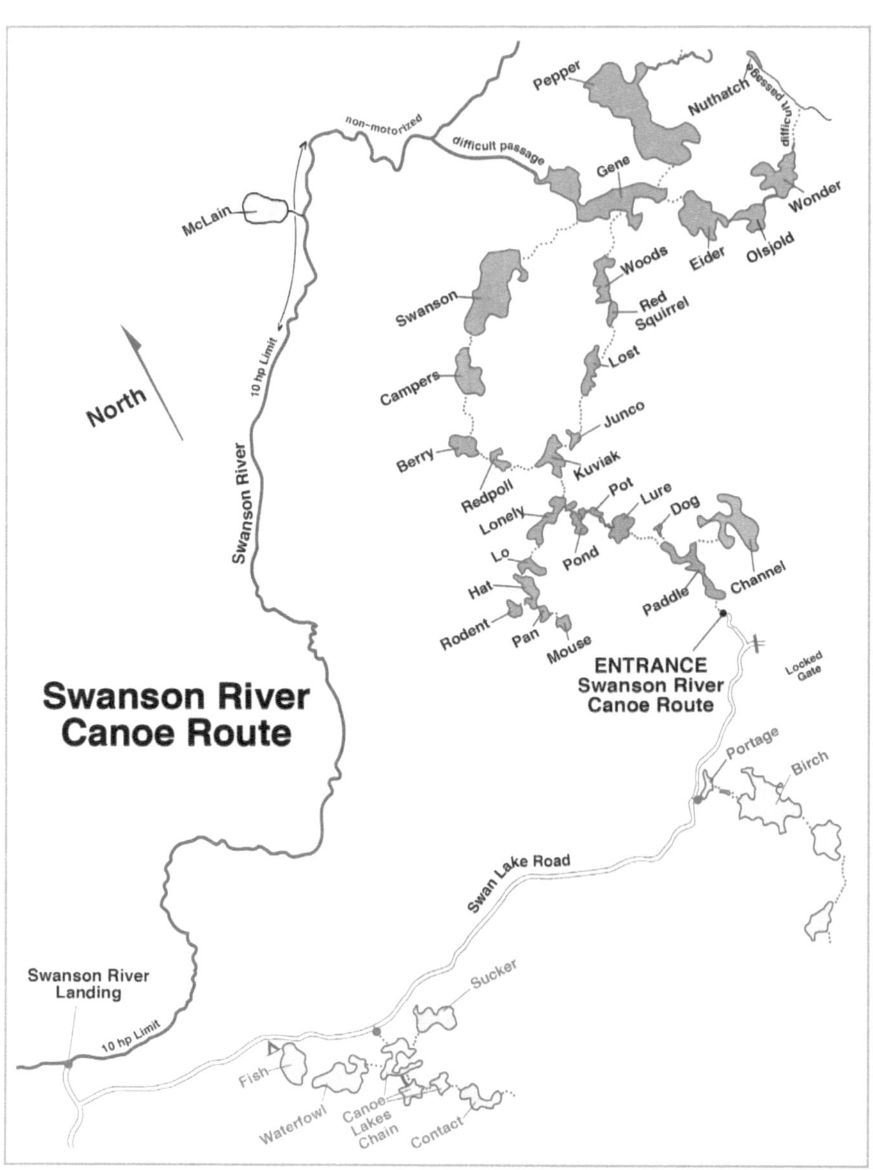

A map of the Swanson River Canoe Area. I put in at Paddle Lake, then tried to reach Gene Lake via the east route, but couldn't find the portage from Woods Lake to Gene Lake. I backtracked and took the west route to Gene Lake. On the way home, I took the creek labeled "difficult passage" north out of Gene Lake and paddled down the Swanson River. In all, I covered 65 miles by foot and canoe.

Alaskan Moose Adventure

When I got laid off, I decided to make the best of the situation and follow a lifelong dream by heading to Alaska for the summer. My friend, Cody, and I road-tripped to the Last Frontier, not knowing whether we were on a two-week vacation or if we would stay the whole summer. As luck would have it, we were privileged to land jobs guiding rafting trips down the Kenai River, seeing bears just about every day and fishing for salmon most evenings.

Just in case we ended up staying, I'd brought my hunting gear along. I've always wanted to shoot a caribou, but there are relatively few on the Kenai Peninsula and permits are available on a lottery basis that I missed out on. But I've always wanted to shoot a moose too, and they are relatively common in that area and you can buy a tag over the counter, so all summer long I plotted and planned how I would kill a moose.

I am a do-it-yourself kind of hunter. I don't want anything handed to me. I could go on a guided hunt, but a guided moose hunt is expensive, plus, I would rather fail on my own than just show up and be the shooter while the guide does all the work. Being from neighboring Wisconsin, I'd heard a lot about moose hunts in Minnesota in which the quintessential hunter roams deep into the Boundary Waters Canoe Area Wilderness with a canoe, a Duluth Pack and rifle to seek his quarry. I'm sort of a romantic in that regard, so that sounded good to me. I decided to do my hunt in the Swanson River Canoe Area, located in the Dave Spencer Unit of the Kenai Wilderness.

All summer I thought about this hunt, but I was behind from the get-go. I followed dead-end lead after dead-end lead trying to get some freezers on Craigslist so I could take my salmon, and potentially moose, home with me, running them via a power inverter hooked up to my truck battery. Once the salmon were in the rivers hot and heavy, appliance stores sold out! I finally tracked down a big chest freezer. It barely fit in the truck!

The rest of the details I foolishly put off until the last minute, then I had to scramble to get everything together. My brother and mom came up for a visit from Aug. 13-20. My last day "working" was Aug. 16 and moose season started Aug. 20. So I had a lot to balance in that timeframe. First off was sighting in my rifle.

The previous deer season I bumped my scope hard on my treestand and knocked it out of alignment, which resulted in two missed deer, and later, a poor hit on another deer that I was luckily able to track down and dispatch. After a few shots, it became apparent that something was wrong with the scope internally. Even when I cranked the elevation down, it kept shooting in the same place. First up for bids, a new scope. Ouch.

I also needed a canoe. Once again, all summer I'd been following leads on Craigslist without results. On Aug. 18, I hastily bought a new scope, the display model canoe and a nonresident moose tag, plus some other moose hunting essentials. I was hemorrhaging money! I'd be lucky to break even on the summer!

The morning of the 19th, I sighted in my scope. I said good-bye to my mom and brother and scrambled to pack a week's worth of gear. I wanted to get into my hunting area a day early, thinking there might be hunting pressure. But getting everything organized took longer than I'd hoped, and I didn't make it to the parking area until 10 p.m. Luckily no one else was there, and the logbook said only one group of canoers had entered the area on the 18th, and none on the 19th. I did see one moose on the drive there. Before I reached the parking lot, I dropped off a bike near the Swanson River Canoe Landing and locked it to a tree in the woods. That way I would have the option of returning to my truck or taking an alternate route back. I spent the night of the 19th sleeping in the back of my truck, eagerly awaiting opening day!

I was up at 5:30 a.m. opening day. I repacked my gear, having dug out my sleeping bag and other gear. Then I packed up and portaged down to the lake. Fog shrouded the still water. Beavers tail slapped. Loons let out lonely cries. It was like something out of a painting. I was nervous about launching in the fog. I had two maps of the area and my GPS, and prior to the trip, I'd gone on Google Earth and tried to figure out where the portage trails were between the lakes. I wasn't so worried about getting lost, but it would simply be difficult to spot moose along the shoreline in the fog.

Out on the lake, the scenery was beautiful. If you'd have blindfolded me and dropped me there, I'd have said I was in the Boundary Waters wilderness in northern Minnesota. Spruce and birch lined the shores. Loons were everywhere. It was the same plants, the same smells and everything like being closer to home. I snapped some cool photos of trumpeter swans

Here's my camp on the first night of my moose hunt in the Swanson River Canoe Area. This was probably the nicest campsite I had during my trip. Each night I set up camp early so I could paddle around, looking for moose in the evening.

appearing on the water like foggy specters. I was taking it in and loving it.

Things changed, however, at the first portage. I am not a big fan of portaging. In fact, I kind of hate it. The first portage turned out to be about 900 yards long. I triple portaged the entire trip, which meant I actually walked the trail five times. On the first trip I carried one pack and a ready rifle. Then I did a trip back empty, then a trip with another pack, another empty trip back, and finally the canoe. That was a lot of mileage. All told, I would log about 65 miles on foot and in the canoe on my moose hunt.

The weather was beautiful for late August in south-central Alaska. This is the rainy season here, but it was sunny and about 70 degrees. Marvelous weather, but I didn't see any moose out and about. I did some fishing, caught some rainbow trout along the lily pads, and before dark, positioned myself overlooking a moosey-looking marsh. Shortly before dark, after not seeing anything, I did some vigorous rubbing on a dead tree with my paddle, trying to simulate the sound of a moose rubbing. A moose hunting DVD I'd bought said this was a good early season technique. It was certainly early in the season, and moose were far from interested in mating at this point.

I didn't see any moose the first day, and despite the great weather, I was pessimistic about the trip. This wasn't good moose-hunting weather. I didn't like portaging. It seems a lot of the successful hunters you hear about call their bulls in during the peak of the rut when they are susceptible to calling. I could hunt for three weeks, but had to leave for my brother's wedding in mid-September and wouldn't be around for the rut. There could be moose all around me in the dense woods, but it seemed I was just banking on the off chance I'd see a moose standing in the open along the lake where I could shoot it. Things weren't looking good. I was starting to feel like this was more of a camping trip than a moose hunt.

On Day 2, I was a little more optimistic about things. So what if I didn't get a moose? I was only planning on being out for a week. I could just enjoy the trip. I decided to stick it out, enjoy the trip, and if I got a moose, fine, and if not, I still had two weeks to formulate a new plan.

Feeling a bit better about the situation, I decided to make a trip out of it. It would be a good story at least and somewhat of an accomplishment. Here I was, alone in the Alaskan wilderness for a week. It was an interesting experience. Day 2 would also be the last time I'd see a person for more than a week. In total, I saw two people on Day 1 and four people on Day 2.

I decided to make Gene Lake my destination. I would do a loop, beginning at Paddle Lake, taking the east entrance in and the west entrance out. According to the pamphlet at the entry point, this would take two to four days. Of course, with hunting as a priority, my schedule was a bit different. I could travel during the day, but needed to have camp set up early so I could hunt in the evenings when the moose were supposed to come out.

On Day 3 I made it to Woods Lake, just before my goal of reaching Gene Lake. I actually set up camp on interconnected Red Squirrel Lake because there was a better campsite there. The lakes are generally small and easy to get around on. Plus, by camping there, I could hunt the marshy shoreline of Woods Lake without disturbing moose.

Day 4 I got ready for the portage into Gene Lake. The night before, I'd had a bad feeling about this. As I hunted that evening, I'd kind of looked around for the portage trailhead. All the trails had been marked with signs thus far. I found no such sign to Gene. In the daylight, I tried again. It should have been a simple matter. According to the map, all I had to do was walk down the edge of an open wet meadow and into the woods. I didn't see any footpaths of those who had done this before. I searched for two hours, even finding a place in the woods that had obviously been

As I paddled around looking for moose, I occupied my time fishing for rainbow trout, which often lurked around the lily pads.

blazed 20 feet wide to accommodate portagers, but the trail simply ended at both ends. Frustrated, the only thing I could do was turn around. I headed back to Junco Lake, feeling cheated and misled by the pamphlet, which clearly stated that this could be done!

On Day 5 I woke up on my campsite on top of the hill between Junco Lake and Kuviak Lake. It had been raining on and off now for the last couple days – weather much more typical of the season. I'd left my canoe and paddle overnight along the shore of Kuviak Lake, since that's where I'd spent the previous night hunting. That morning, I walked down to the shore next to the canoe in desperate need of a bath. With my bath complete, I headed back up the hill 125 yards to my tent. I cooked breakfast, broke camp and portaged my first bag to the canoe. To my amazement, my paddle, which just an hour ago was fine, was now in two pieces! It was dotted with holes as if someone had peppered it with a shotgun, but I found no pellets, nor heard any gunshot. Could a bear have chewed it in half? There were no uniform jaw imprints. I was dumbfounded. Luckily, it didn't break straight in half, but rather, in two long splinters. I was able to duct tape it back together, and although you wouldn't want to make any power strokes with it, it was quite functional.

So now I weighed my options. I'd wasted a couple days trying to get to a lake I couldn't reach. My paddle was broken. I was behind schedule. I still hadn't gotten even a glimpse of a moose. Should I just head for home? No one would blame me. I had tried. That's when my stubbornness kicked in. Doggone it! I had set out to reach Gene Lake. I didn't care so much about the moose hunt anymore. It was now about this journey and setting goals for myself. I decided to keep going.

My goal for the day was to try to reach Gene Lake, or at least Swanson Lake, via the west route. According to literature I'd read, those two lakes had good moose habitat along their shorelines. Campers Lake, however, was not mentioned.

For a while now, I had been thinking, I'd just like to see a moose, even a cow and calf. Something! Paddling to the north side of Campers Lake on the sunny afternoon of Day 5, I heard rustling in the brush. Seconds later, a cow moose poked her head out about 100 yards away. Finally! It had taken me five days to see a moose. They are truly incredible animals. In this area, a legal moose is any bull that is has unbranched spike antlers, has an antler spread of 50 inches or more, or has at least three brow tines on one antler. (And people back home thing the regulations are complicated!) Before my trip, my "goal" was something middle of the road. I wanted something with some nice paddles, but I didn't know how badly I wanted a 70-inch giant and the associated weight. At this point, however, the first spike I saw was going to die, and I was trying hard to grow some antlers on this moose!

After a couple minutes of watching me, the cow retreated to the brush. That settled it! I made a short hike to Swanson Lake, which supposedly had better moose cover, but I liked what I saw on Campers Lake better, even before I'd seen the moose. I set up camp back on the south shore of Campers Lake where the wind would be in my favor in the evening.

That night, I was fishing on a beautiful evening with that perfect golden sunlight filtering down when I heard a splash across the lake. I turned and saw a moose in the water! It looked like a cow, but I wanted to be sure. I retreated around a point, then crept up deathly silent on the moose in my canoe, shielded by a small island. My heart was pounding as I rounded the final spit of land. There were now two moose: a cow and a calf. I let out a deep breath. Talk about excitement! I took some video of them and just watched for a while. I have a feeling it was the same cow I'd seen earlier in the day and her calf just hadn't poked its nose out earlier. Either way, it

On the fifth day of the hunt, I broke camp and hiked to my canoe, only to find my paddle broken in half. It was peppered with holes. I'll never know what really happened, but I assume a bear bit it in half. Luckily, it didn't break cleanly, but rather, in long splinters that I was able to duct tape together.

felt good to see some moose!

Day 6 I made it into Gene Lake. Each lake along the way seemed to get more beautiful, and finally, for the first time since the first day, I saw something that told me I wasn't in Minnesota – mountains in the distance. The portage into Gene had been the longest yet at nearly a mile, and I was rewarding myself for a job well done. I felt as if getting to the lake was my actual purpose. I was now more concerned with the trip itself, and the hunt seemed secondary.

Despite all those good vibes, there was a dark side. I'd planned to be out for seven days. My supplies were running low. Earlier, I'd been eating a lot of oatmeal mixed with chocolate chips and peanut butter. It's quick, easy, tasty and doesn't require cooking. I kept eating that and neglected cooking. I saved one last meal of this for the long trip out down the Swanson River, as there wouldn't be anywhere to cook along the way. There were other problems. My water filtration device was now clogged and I couldn't pump fresh water. I now had to rely on boiling. And the fuel for my cook stove was almost empty. I had enough gas left for about two meals, and they'd have to be quick ones. I needed to cook over more fires, but it kept raining and everything was wet. So I had food, but it was tough to eat. Water was all around me, but it was tough to drink. Quite the paradox.

Despite that, it was a beautiful night on Gene Lake. It was that perfect golden sunlight again. I took lots of pictures, but I'd like to see what a nature photographer who knows what he's doing could have done with that lighting! I paddled around the lake a little bit, looking for the portage trails to the next lakes and the river route out. I fished a little, but it seemed the more I tried to be quiet, the more I banged stuff around in the bottom of my canoe. There was no way I was going to see a moose!

About 9 p.m., I was heading slowly back to camp. I came around an island, and standing in the marshy grass of the mainland was a moose! My first thought was it looked like there were two of them, with one in back of the other. A split-second later, I realized it wasn't another moose, but antlers! Now my heart was pounding!

I'd already deemed myself far too unsteady to shoot from a canoe. My predetermined plan was to get to land and a rest upon seeing a moose. Luckily my green canoe probably blended well with the grass, and the moose didn't notice me at first. I jumped into knee-deep water, wearing jeans and hiking boots, and scrambled to find a suitable rest. It was brushy here, and all I had was a sapling that had actually been bent over by a feeding moose. Now, about that rack. It was sure decent, but I didn't think it would go 50 inches. I decided to count brow tines, reminding myself to beware of shreds of velvet hanging down that could deceive me. In the low light, it was sure hard to tell, but it looked like he had three brow tines on the right side. I counted again. Three. Again. Three. He was legal! Now my heart was really hammering! A moose is a huge target, but I was shaking so badly, I couldn't even keep my cross-hairs on the front half of his body. I told myself over and over to relax. There was no way I could take a shot like this. I clicked the safety off, then put it back on. I looked at the bull again, took off the safety again and put it back on again. I told myself I was just watching a moose, that's all. I tried and tried to calm down, but I just couldn't. I watched the moose for a couple minutes. He had heard my splashing and was staring in my direction, which is actually the reason I was able to see his brow tines in the first place. He was in a wet meadow, about 15 yards from the lake and about 20 yards from the trees. Finally, the moose stepped toward the brush. "Oh no you don't!" I thought. "There

On the sixth evening of my hunt, I saw this bull standing in a wet meadow near the water's edge. Despite a terrible case of "bull fever," I made a lucky shot and dropped him in his tracks. The bull was in full velvet and sported 17 points and a 42-inch spread. He carried three brow tines on each antler, which made him legal.

is no way I'm letting you get away!" He stopped right away, seemingly unconcerned, but now I was getting anxious. The golden sky from earlier in the evening had shrouded over with clouds. I prayed out loud over and over, "Please God, help me calm down. Help me be steady!" And then, as if in answer to my prayer, just at that moment, a single shaft of golden light streamed down out of the clouds. It was a transcendent moment. If that's not proof that God exists, I don't know what is.

I wasn't letting the moose go any farther. Before I had time to really think about it, the gun went off. I raced to recover from the recoil and get ready for a follow-up shot. I was only shooting a .270 Win., plus, my confidence in my shooting ability in that wired state was not high. I struggled to find the running moose in my scope, but there was no moose in sight. And there was no sound of splashing water. And then it dawned on me. "Oh … my … gosh," I thought. "I just killed a moose!"

I jumped in the canoe, paddling so frantically you could have water-skied behind me. However, my paced slowed greatly as I approached the shore. I was now very nervous about what I might find. An injured moose would not be very happy to see me!

Within two minutes, I'd reached the shoreline. I'd marked the spot, even before the shot, by two dead trees in the background. And then, there he was, velvet antler sticking up in the air, stone dead.

I approached very nervously, rifle at the ready, but he was dead. Had I been shooting at a target, it would have been deemed a terrible shot. I was aiming at the front shoulder, but actually hit the moose in the neck, right in the vertebrae, rendering an instant death. No grass was disturbed by his feet. He hadn't even kicked! It was a terrible shot on paper, but a perfect shot in practice!

The GPS revealed two things: 1. The shot had been 189 yards. And 2. The moose dropped 542 yards from where I stopped bushwhacking two days earlier when I tried to reach Gene Lake from the east entrance!

I stood over the bull in awe and just looked at him. He had 17 points and a 42-inch spread. Most importantly, he had three brow tines on each antler, making him legal.

A few days before the hunt I'd gone horseback riding, and as I looked at the horses, I tried to envision them as moose. I think this guy was bigger than the horses! I took a bunch of photos, but with darkness falling, I decided to leave him for the night and get a fresh start in the morning. He fell 780 yards from my tent.

I didn't get much sleep that night. I was definitely excited, but I was thinking a lot about the task of butchering the moose by myself. I've cut up enough deer to understand anatomy, but this would be on an industrial-sized scale. And then what about a mount? I'd never even caped a deer before. Should I cape the moose? Decisions, decisions. Sleep didn't come easily.

The next morning, Day 7, I think I was up fairly early. I'd been turning on my cell phone sparingly, since there was no reception anyway, and that's all I had for a clock, and the battery was now dead. I paddled back to the moose, very relieved to find that no critters had disturbed him overnight. And then it was down to business. He fell in ankle-deep water, so I just wore the same wet clothes from the day before, trying to preserve my dry clothes as best I could in the rainy weather.

Things went pretty well, I think. I removed the hindquarter, then skinned up, keeping the cape intact. The moose fell in a grassy meadow, but luckily there were a couple dead trees, and with about 80 feet of rope and a come-along, I was able to flip him over.

I estimate it took me about eight or nine hours to butcher the moose. In

I took a break from butchering the moose to snap this photo. I had skinned the top of the hide and then used a come-along to winch the top hindquarter "against the grain" to remove it from the ball-and-socket joint.

the canoe were now several hundred pounds of moose meat, a giant head and cape, and lil' ol' me. And that's with most of my gear back in camp! There was *not* much freeboard and I paddled back to camp *very* carefully!

I really wanted to get going and get a jump on getting out. The plan was to take the creek ominously labeled "difficult passage" on the map coming out the north side of Gene Lake. After paddling 1.25 miles down the creek, it would be an easy 19-mile float down the Swanson River to the waiting bicycle, then a 12-mile pedal to the truck. Great plan in theory! I left the moose quarters propped across the gunwales to cool, then enjoyed some moose tenderloins over a fire and boiled up some water for my Nalgene bottle on what I assumed would be my last night camping.

On Day 8 I began my trip down the little creek. It didn't look too bad at first. A beaver dam blocked the entrance right away, so I had to unload everything from the canoe, pull the canoe over the dam and reload it. This is *not* fun. After reloading all the gear, I carefully climbed into the rear seat and began paddling down the creek. I'd made it about 20 yards when the canoe ground to a halt on a shallow gravel bar. I had no choice but to bail out, grab the front handle of the canoe, lunge backwards and yank the canoe along one step at a time. After a few yards, the canoe was floating again, and I climbed back in.

After another short paddle, I bottomed out again. I quickly learned it didn't pay to ride in the canoe because the creek was too narrow and there were too many obstacles. There would be a stretch of 20 yards of water deep enough to float a boat, but then there would be a gravel bar and I would have to yank the canoe, with all that weight in it, over it. It was brutal, but the map declared the creek was only 1.25 miles long. It still sounded better than multiple portages back the way I'd came, especially considering I knew the first portage was a mile and I'd have to walk it several times.

As I got farther downstream, those 20-yard stretches became 10-yard stretches. I was getting across these rocks by simply bending down, yanking the canoe a foot, taking a step back and repeating as often as necessary with a fully loaded canoe. Not easy work! Plus, with cooking time and ability running low, all I ate all day long were two packs of Raman noodles for breakfast, my last serving of oatmeal and two granola bars. I drank my bottle of water, but it wasn't enough.

When I got into the woods, deadfalls were added to the mix. Then I had the privilege of unloading all the gear, sliding the canoe over the fallen log, then reloading.

At this point I did some scouting. This was excruciating work. Earlier I'd wished I'd had someone along just to experience the beauty and fun of this trip. Now I wouldn't wish it on my worst enemy.

Scouting revealed six deadfalls across the creek in the woods, then a meadow with deeper water. It was reckoning time. The moose head, cape and antlers were heavy and the cape had to be at least four feet long. I could not lift it, and rather, had to simply drag it. I couldn't go on like this. A head mount would be great, but I didn't know if I could physically get the head and cape out of the woods. With some regret, I got the saw out. That first saw stroke was painful to make, because at that point I knew I'd ruined my head mount. After that it went better, although it's no fun trying to saw the rack off a moose skull. Incredibly, as the saw cut through on the final stroke, the blade snapped in half! Had this happened just a few strokes earlier, I'd have ruined the mount, but would have been forced to carry the entire skull anyway!

The meadow went better, but there were still a lot of gravel bars. When

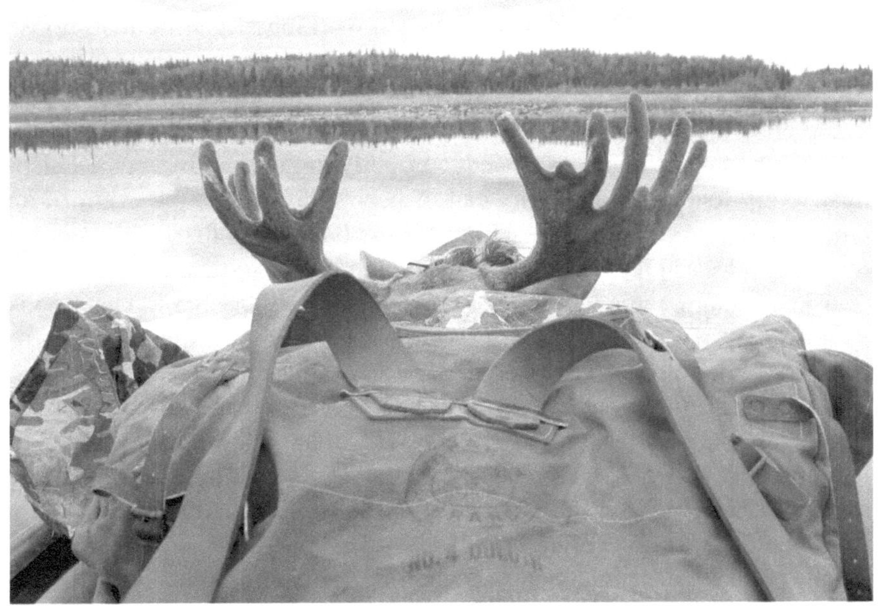

A velvet rack and a Duluth Pack riding atop a load of moose meat in my canoe.

I got into the woods again, the water was ankle deep. The canoe would not float, so I literally lurched it along one foot at a time for about two-tenths of a mile. The pamphlet at the landing said it took about 9 to 11 hours to go from Gene Lake to the Swanson River Canoe Landing. First off, I find that unrealistic even for people who aren't hauling moose, and even without the moose, this route was absolutely miserable!

As I strained and toiled, I thought about the little things back home that I missed: eating a pizza, hanging out with friends, petting a cat. Little stuff like that kept my mind distracted while I labored, and it gave me something to shoot for and a reason to go on. I worried a little. I prayed a lot. One twisted ankle, one bad cut and I was in serious trouble. I had no first-aid kit and no way to communicate with anyone, except maybe an airplane. Food and water were running low. I began to wonder, at what point do I simply dump the meat and just get out of here with my life?

After more than a week without human contact, and with an incredible amount of physical exertion on very little food and water, I was starting to lose it. I talked to myself constantly. I yelled at the sticks that scraped along the side of the canoe, then taunted them when I made it past them without them dumping my load. I knew I was right on the edge of a breakdown, but what could I do? I just kept on working at getting that moose down the creek.

After about 14 hours of effort and with darkness falling, I had no choice but to erect the tent on a grassy spot just big enough for it right next to the canoe, which once again, was wedged tightly in the river by rocks. I slept next to my loaded rifle and my can of bear spray, but in the event of an emergency, I would not be reaching for the bear spray first! This was *my* moose and I was prepared to kill anything that tried to take it from me!

I knew that evening I had enough fuel for one last burn. The woods were too wet for building a fire. Would it be food or water? I compromised. I boiled up my last pack of Raman noodles and left it overnight. The next morning, when everything had cooled, I carefully poured the water from the noodles into my water bottle. It was a little cloudy, but with a liberal dose of Kool-Aid powder, who knew? I had 14 ounces of water. I ate the Raman, but I wasn't hungry. Still, I knew I needed it. The only dry food I had left was one granola bar.

I'd planned the night before to be out of this hellhole, but I'd only lugged the canoe 1 mile in 14 hours. I still had a quarter-mile to go. Although I hadn't planned to camp, I had been lucky to keep some of my clothes dry. The clothes I'd been wearing were soaked from the creek and from the rain. The last dry clothes I had left had been a great comfort for sleep that night. When I woke up, it was hard to bend my fingers. Calluses had erupted where all my fingers met my palms. It hurt to hold things.

I did a little scouting on the morning of Day 9. I only had about a quarter-mile to go to get to the river, but it was the worst stretch yet. The river was just a trickle barely wide enough to get a canoe through. My only option was to load the meat into my backpack, a quarter at a time, and hike it all downstream to where I could float again. I made six trips, getting all but the larger hindquarter downstream. That quarter had some extra pelvic bones and simply wouldn't fit in the backpack (later, I found out it weighed 95 pounds). I was able to fight it downstream in the boat. After 14 hours on Day 8 and about six more hours on Day 9, I finally reached the Swanson River!

The river itself is more of a creek by my standards, and it was a windy little bugger. It was choked with lily pads and other vegetation, and the heavily loaded canoe plowed along. The creek wound through vast wet meadows with thick spruce forests along the edges. Three times I saw

After spending an entire day butchering my moose, I enjoyed moose tenderloins over the fire on what I assumed would be my last night in the wilderness. I had no clue how difficult getting the bull out of the woods would be!

smoking-fresh moose rubs on spruce trees as I paddled. My moose had hardened antlers, but hadn't stripped any velvet. He was probably just days away from doing so.

Now I wasn't working as hard, and my rain-soaked cotton shirt was like a cold pack wrapped around my torso. I knew I'd be hypothermic if I kept at it. I retrieved my high-tech long john top from my bag and it was like sitting in front of a fire. It instantly dried me out and warmed me up, and with my old beat-up duck coat – my final dry item – on top, I felt better instantly.

Progress was slow in the weeds, but at least I was floating! Of course, it couldn't be smooth sailing the whole way! I had to unload the canoe to get over a couple beaver dams and a couple more fallen trees. Plus, there were a few scattered boulder fields where I bottomed out. Then it was back to the old familiar routine of get out, yank, drain water from pants as much as possible, and get back in. It was not the "easy flatwater float" as advertised in the pamphlet, but it was still a lot better than that hellish creek!

I estimate I started down the river at 6 p.m. on Day 9. At the logbook, I indicated I planned to be out for seven days. I was already two days overdue, and frankly, I wanted to be *out* of there! I made up my mind I was not camping another night, and plus, with all the wet meadows along the river, there really was no place to camp anyway.

By nightfall, I had paddled 11 miles downriver, according to the GPS. I had 8 miles to go. It was a cloudy night with no moon to guide me. I continued onward. Luck was with me and all the beaver dams and deadheads were behind me. I only had to get out of the canoe one time in the darkness to wrench the boat over a rock.

The paddle in the dark wasn't too bad. I thought back to all the mornings I'd paddled out before dawn to go duck hunting. This really was no different. A couple times I encountered backwater areas and I had to shine a light into the water to reveal which direction the weeds bent so I knew which way was downstream, but I was going the right way. Despite the fact this was a river, the current was negligible and it was basically like paddling across a lake. I was taking numerous breaks now. I was yawning a lot. Amazingly, I wasn't sore anywhere from the previous day's arduous canoe dragging – just my hands. Tonight, however, the paddling was getting to me and my shoulders were aching. I took a few breaks, but I reminded myself resting didn't get me any closer to being out of there.

Everything after dark was smooth sailing. If there would have been a fallen log, I probably would have had no choice but to wait until daylight to cross it. My final challenge came just three-quarters of a mile from the takeout! Up ahead on this otherwise quiet creek, I heard rushing water. I paddled up to it in the darkness, held myself on a rock, and flipped on the flashlight. I'd have to get down a small chute. Normally this would be no big deal. Fun even. But not when you've got a person, gear and an entire moose in a canoe, in the dark no less! To run the chute, which was maybe a 2-foot drop, I had to hit the center, then make a quick left turn to get around some rocks. It would be tricky even in the daylight. A fallen tree on the left side didn't help either. I weighed my options. I was so close to getting out! I just wanted to be home! I didn't know how much longer it would be until daylight. I didn't want to wait, but I risked dumping everything, losing everything and taking a cold swim with no dry clothes. It was not a good situation. I flipped on the light again. I memorized the route. Then I backed up, turned the bow downstream and held my breath.

The canoe nosed into the gap of the chute. I dug hard on the left side, swinging the nose around. The canoe dropped down onto a flat rock below, paused, then popped free. I shot out toward the left bank, free and quite upright! Some sincere words of thanks were uttered!

I reached the landing, I learned later, at 4:30 a.m. on the 10th day of

I took a self-timer photo with the fully loaded canoe as I shoved off from camp on Gene Lake to begin the arduous paddle down the creek. I'm still smiling in this photo, but I wouldn't be in a few hours.

the trip. The 1.25-mile creek run was done. The 19-mile river float was behind me. All I had to do was retrieve the bike from the woods, then ride 12 miles back to the truck! I poked into the woods, flashlight in hand, and nosed around. I had come down this little trail, I recalled, then turned left, toward the river, and locked the bike to the tree. I couldn't find it! Where was it? It had to be here! I'd thought of everything. I'd marked the landing on my GPS, why didn't I mark the bike? Ugh! After a half-hour of searching, with no clue how much longer until sunrise, I decided to start walking. I figured it would take me four hours to reach the truck. It was not an option I was looking forward to, but I couldn't just stand around, soaked from the waist down, waiting for sunrise.

The road into this area is a 29-mile-long stretch of gravel. You would have no business being down here if you weren't hunting, fishing or camping. It doesn't get a lot of traffic. So you can imagine my utter amazement when, a half-mile into my hike, I saw headlights slicing through the blackness behind me! I turned, stood in the middle of the road and put both hands in the air. A minivan with a canoe on top pulled to a stop.

"There isn't any chance you could give me a ride to Paddle Lake, could you?" I pleaded. Paddle Lake is the very last stop along the road, right before a gate blocks further progress.

"That's actually where we're heading," the driver said. "Geez, what are you doing out here this time of day walking down the road? Hop in!"

No better sound had ever reached my ears! The two guys said they were on their way to go moose hunting. I told them that I'd shot a bull and it was down at the Swanson Landing and I just needed to shuttle around with my truck.

"I can tell," one guy piped up. "You smell like moose."

Indeed I did. The smell of moose permeated my clothes, my bags, everything. It was actually starting to make me sick.

The guys were good company, but we all commented on how long the drive seemed. This made me extra glad of my good fortune in getting a ride. Back at my truck, we talked for a few minutes. I told them I'd seen just three moose in 10 days. They didn't like the sound of that, especially considering one of them was dead. I told them not to shoot one too far back in, and they assured me they weren't going far. I'd have gladly given them some money, but my wallet was back in the canoe. I thanked them again and again, then was on my way.

Now, being inactive for the first time in hours, aches crept up in my body everywhere. It hurt to walk. My callused hands were cracked and bloody. It hurt like crazy to wrap my fingers around anything and pick it up. I'd left an unopened energy drink in my truck, and I'd thought about it all day, but my throat was so dry, it was painful to swallow. In my condition, I didn't know how I'd load everything in the truck.

Back at the canoe landing, I started with the small stuff first. It was like stretching before an athletic event. When I could move a small bag, I upgraded to a larger one, then a larger one. I could only get the truck within about 50 yards of the canoe landing. The last thing in the canoe was the larger hindquarter. I was sprinting toward the truck and losing my grip on it, but I flopped it onto the tailgate and breathed heavily. With the canoe shoved in the back of the truck, I had one task left: to find that bike! It would have been one thing to lose my own bike, but it was borrowed! Now, at 6:30 a.m., there was enough light to see, and I managed to find it after about 15 minutes. Next time I will mark it on my GPS!

I drove into town, bent on eating at a small café. It was closed. Just as well. I couldn't swallow anyway. The night before as I paddled, all this stomach acid, with nothing to digest all day but a pack of Raman and a granola bar, kept sloshing around and giving me heartburn – something I rarely get. Today when I finally did eat something, not only was it painful to swallow, but it burned in my chest, too.

I went to the grocery store instead. I couldn't even carry the basket in my hands. I had to carry it in the crook of my elbow. I washed my hands but it hurt too much to rub them together. I walked around the store with a hollow look in my sagging eyes, slouched over and walking like an old man, but I didn't care.

And now, with moose meat in my freezer, my hunt is complete. What they say about moose hunting is right: "the work doesn't start until the moose is on the ground."

I knew the last couple days that I would always cherish this hunt, but it was something I wanted to look back on, not still be experiencing. The last couple days were sheer hell. It tested me both mentally and physically. There were times I thought about leaving the meat. There were times I thought about flagging down an airplane. There were times when I wondered if I would die of hypothermia, or dehydration or starvation. There were even times when I looked at the rifle and thought there was an easy way out. But I wouldn't trade this experience for anything in the world, and now that it's over, I can take the time to look back and appreciate it. It has made me a better person. It has helped me believe in myself. It has shown me I can do things I didn't think I could do. It has given me a sense of accomplishment and an appreciation for all the little things in everyday life that I so often take for granted. I'm sure as I reflect back on it all, in time, I will learn many other things. But for right now, I think I need a nap. Thank you all for reading.

Joe Shead
Aug. 29, 2009

A condensed version of this story appeared in the July 2010 issue of Fur-Fish-Game.

Postscript:
I wrote this story the same day I got the moose out of the woods. After returning to my summer cabin, I put the moose meat in the freezer, then hammered out the entire story before I went to bed. But as I was about to learn, the story was far from over! Read on for the rest of the story.

Alaskan Moose Adventure: The Rest of the Story

I didn't get my moose back to civilization until four days after I shot it. It took one day of butchering and three excruciating days trying to fight the moose down a creek and then a river. Luckily, the game bags kept the bugs at bay and the weather stayed cool enough that the meat was fine. In fact, I had promised my boss at the rafting company that I'd give him a quarter if I shot a moose, and he hung his quarter in a shed for a few more days to tenderize it.

Before I returned to my summer cabin, however, I swung by a taxidermist's shop to see what could be done about a mount. Honestly, I hate velvet. I never wanted to shoot anything in velvet, but I took what I could get and I was stuck with it. I'd have greatly preferred a nice polished, chocolate rack, but since I shot the bull in velvet, I decided I should try to preserve it the way it was when I shot it. I'd encased each antler in a cloth game bag to protect the velvet and to keep insects out. When I reached the taxidermist, first he was impressed that I'd killed the moose where I did. The population in that area had been declining. His next question was why hadn't I brought the rack to him sooner? I could have killed him for that comment!

I asked him to do what he could to preserve the velvet and explained that I needed a quick turnaround because I had to get home to Wisconsin soon. He made no promises, given that it had been a few days and the blood within the velvet may have spoiled, but he said he'd see what he could do.

A week later, I got a call that the rack was ready. The taxidermist did what he could to preserve the velvet, but warned me that it needed time to air out. It definitely smelled like chemicals! He advised me to hang the rack in a garage when I got home to let it air out where it would be safe from insects. He also said that it may have been too far gone and the velvet may go bad, which it did. Ultimately, after hanging the rack in the garage over the winter, I ended up stripping off the velvet the following spring.

Me with the velvet moose rack after I got it back from the taxidermist.

After the moose hunt, I just treaded water for a week or so, recuperating, fishing, hunting spruce grouse and picking berries. Cody had flown home already to take some classes, so I was alone. My brother, Jack, who had just been here the week before the moose hunt, flew back up to drive home with me. Jack is a mechanic, and I have very limited mechanical skills, so I suspect my parents sent him, lest I break down in the middle of the Yukon or something. Either way, I was happy for the company on the four-day, 3,600-mile drive home!

We spent a few days fishing before we departed. Incredibly, one day, as we drove over a bridge, we spotted a bull moose standing in the river. We stopped to look at it, then we asked each other the $6 million question: was he legal? I'd estimate his spread was 48 inches, but I don't know if it would hit that magic 50-inch mark that would make him a legal bull. It didn't matter now, but man, at just 100 yards off the road, the moose would have been a *lot* easier to pack out! Plus he was out of velvet!

After a few days of fishing, it was time to hit the highway. We needed the drive to go smoothly because our brother, James, was getting married in Milwaukee in a week and we were both in the wedding. And that's partly where the trouble started. Normally, I drive the speed limit, but I wanted to make time and was hot-footing it a bit. That's when I got pulled over by a state trooper. The trooper was nice enough. I admitted I'd been going a little fast and he just gave me a warning. He asked if I'd been hunting (perhaps he'd seen the moose antlers through my truck topper?) and I said I had. He asked if he might look at the rack. I had nothing to hide and I was awfully proud of my hard-earned moose, so I showed him the rack.

"Where's your locking metal tag?" he asked.

"What metal tag?" I responded.

"Big-game animals need to have a metal tag around the antlers," he replied.

I hadn't received a metal tag when I bought my license. In fact, I had intended to buy my license at a sporting goods store, where I knew the employees would know what they were doing. But as it turned out, crunched for time, I bought my license at Walmart and the kid behind the counter struggled. It took him 45 minutes to issue me my license!

"I can't enforce wildlife violations, but if I were you, I wouldn't go across the border without that metal tag," the trooper advised as he walked back to his squad before he got back on the road.

Now what? I'm a law-abiding citizen. I hadn't done anything wrong! Or certainly I wouldn't *try* to do anything wrong! A knot formed in my stomach. What should we do?

We had time to think about it. The towns are pretty spread out when you get north of Anchorage. When we got to Tok – the last town before the Canadian border – we decided to call the Alaska Dept. of Fish and Game.

I explained the situation over the phone. The closest wildlife trooper was very interested in my story. He was an hour away but told me to sit tight because he wanted to investigate this. Great. Jack and I ducked into a restaurant, where Jack ate his fill while I picked at my food.

Finally, the trooper arrived. I told my story and showed him my moose.

"Right now you have an illegally tagged moose," he explained. "I can take your moose, your gun, everything."

I told him I wasn't trying to pull anything. I'd bought the license and had cut out a corner on the paper tag like I was supposed to. I simply hadn't been issued this green metal tag he kept talking about.

He went back inside his squad to make some calls.

In the meantime, Jack and I talked while knots formed ever-tighter in my stomach. Jack had gone to police academy and had briefly done water patrol for the sheriff's department and served as a bailiff.

"Your story is believable," Jack said. "All your mannerisms point to the fact you're telling the truth. Your palms are up, you are freely showing him your paperwork and your moose. If I were in his shoes, I'd know you had made an honest mistake."

That made me feel a little better, but it was ultimately the trooper's decision.

After an agonizingly long time, he came back from his squad.

"I was on the phone with Walmart in Anchorage," he said. "They said they sold four nonresident moose tags, but they don't have any paperwork that shows you bought a moose license there."

Gulp.

"Then I called licensing in Juneau," he continued. "They don't have you in the system either."

"Well I bought my license," I insisted. "I do have the little paper card with the date notched out. If I don't have the metal tag, it's because they didn't give it to me when I bought it. Here, I even have the receipt that says I bought the license," I offered, pulling this new piece of evidence from my wallet.

This got the trooper's interest. It was undeniable. There it was, a Walmart receipt for a hunting license for $400 – the amount of a non-resident moose license. I had no credit card trail because I'd used my tip money and paid cash for it, but I had the receipt.

"Hmm," the trooper said as he studied the paperwork. "Maybe we could pull the security footage and see if you really were at the counter."

"Go ahead!" I pleaded. "There ought to be plenty of it! The kid who sold me the license had no idea what he was doing. I was there for 45 minutes!"

I don't know if the trooper ever did check the security footage, but the receipt had turned the tides. In fact, that receipt is what saved me, or I'm pretty sure I'd have never gotten to keep that moose and I probably would have paid a pretty hefty fine.

The trooper told me to call licensing in Juneau, explain the situation and get their blessing before crossing the border. With that, he left. But at least he left me with my moose!

It was after office hours, so Jack and I had no choice but to spend the night. Jack thought he could wriggle up and sleep across the dash of my truck. He couldn't. So we both tried to sleep sitting up in my regular-cab pickup. I'm sure Jack got a lot more sleep than I did!

The following day I was on the phone with licensing in Juneau and with Walmart and Fish and Game in Anchorage. After explaining the situation and giving the trooper's reference report information, I finally got everyone's blessing to keep the moose and go home ... as long as I purchased a $5 replacement metal tag! Ugh! That I did, and it will never come off that rack! And I can promise you, one of the first things I did when I got home was to chew out the manager at Walmart, who sent me a measly $25 gift card for my trouble.

After all that, we were on the road. We breezed through customs both entering Canada and then entering the United States in North Dakota, which makes me wonder if I hadn't gotten pulled over for speeding, would I have ever had any trouble, or were we just lucky to have the right border agents that day?

We made it to Milwaukee without incident, but I let some of the details of our predicament slip before the wedding. I received a lot of questions from interested friends and family that day! I was just really glad I was at the wedding and not in jail in Alaska!

After the moose hunt, I swore I'd never do it again, but you know how time has a way of healing wounds! The next summer, I was leading rafting trips down the Kenai River again and I got thinking about that moose hunt. But it turns out the taxidermist had been right about declining moose numbers in my hunt area. In fact, that area was now closed to nonresident moose hunting, and the unit had been changed from a three-brow minimum to a four-brow minimum! Had I gotten to Alaska one year later, I'd have never been able to embark on my moose adventure, and even if I could have, the bull I shot would no longer have been legal! I guess things worked out after all, although if that zone had been closed, it would have saved me a lot of agony!

I also learned some other information about that zone. The nonresident success rate in my zone the year of my hunt was a scant 17 percent. I had beaten the odds just to shoot a moose, even before I beat the odds getting him back home!